PAGEMAKER® 6.0

FOR WINDOWS® 95 AND MACINTOSH®

PageMaker® 6.0

For Windows® 95 and Macintosh®

WILLIAM R. PASEWARK, SR., PH.D.
Professor Emeritus, Texas Tech University
Office Management Consultant

JOIN US ON THE INTERNET
WWW: http://www.thomson.com
EMAIL: findit@kiosk.thomson.com A service of I(T)P®

South-Western Educational Publishing
an International Thomson Publishing company I(T)P®

Cincinnati • Albany, NY • Belmont, CA • Bonn • Boston • Detroit • Johannesburg • London • Madrid
Melbourne • Mexico City • New York • Paris • Singapore • Tokyo • Toronto • Washington

I(T)P™

International Thomson Publishing

South-Western Educational Publishing is a division of International Thomson Publishing, Inc. The ITP trademark is used under license.

ISBN: 0-538-71639-8

1 2 3 4 5 6 7 8 BN 2 1 0 9 8 7 6

Printed in the United States of America

Editor in Chief: *Robert E. First*

Managing Editor: *Janie Schwark*

Marketing Manager: *Kent Christensen*

Production Coordinator: *Jane Congdon*

Editor: *Angela McDonald*

Senior Quality Assurance Specialist: *Michael Jackson*

Development and Production: *Custom Editorial Productions, Inc.*

To the Student

PageMaker 6.0 is a popular desktop publishing program that provides you with the tools you need to create attractive and stimulating publications. This program can be used to produce newsletters, letterheads, business cards, invitations, and many other types of documents. Desktop publishing software is used in personal, academic, career, and business settings to produce publications quickly and professionally.

PageMaker 6.0 for Windows and Macintosh: QuickTorial provides a complete and successful learning experience for you. Objectives listed at the beginning of each lesson give you an overview of the lesson. Short segments of text explain PageMaker features and how they are used. Then hands-on exercises guide you through the various computer operations. These exercises give you a chance to practice the concepts you have just learned. The book includes many illustrations and exercises to simplify complex concepts and operations. End-of-lesson activities and exercises help reinforce the concepts learned.

The following conventions are used in this book:

- *Keying* means entering text into a computer. The terms *keying* and *typing* are sometimes used interchangeably.
- Text that you are to key is in bold type.
- File names are bold.
- Key terms and words in the book that refer to what you see on the screen are in italics.
- Commands or functions that you are to perform are in bold.
- The + sign between commands means to hold down the first key, press the second key, and release the two keys simultaneously.

To the Teacher

Students enter computer courses with widely varying levels of skill and knowledge. Some may already know several software programs; others may have limited computer experience. *PageMaker 6.0 for Windows and Macintosh: QuickTorial* is designed to help all students develop computer competency using a desktop publishing program.

This book has been structured to encourage a mastery level of learning. It follows the Madeline Hunter model that consists of input, modeling, guided practice, and independent practice before a final check for mastery is completed. Exercises can be treated as guided practices and review exercises as independent practice. Review questions check for the students' understanding of content. Lesson 12 can be used as a final check for mastery.

preface

Average completion time for the book is 12–15 hours but will vary depending on the student's ability and previous computer experience. This book is appropriate for students in a variety of educational settings, including high schools, community colleges, continuing education programs, vocational technical schools, career colleges, weekend courses, adult education programs, and personal instruction. The reading level and instructional pattern make it appropriate for a wide variety of learners.

System Requirements

Windows

- 486-based DOS-compatible computer (Pentium recommended)
- Microsoft Windows 3.1 (Windows 95 recommended)
- 10 megabytes (MB) of RAM memory for Windows 3.1 (16 MB recommended)
- 8 MB of RAM memory for Windows 95
- VGA display card (24-bit or greater Super VGA or XGA recommended)
- Mouse or pointing device
- 24 MB of free hard disk space (40 MB recommended)
- High-density disk drive (CD-ROM recommended)

Macintosh

- 68030 or greater processor (68040 or PowerPC recommended)
- System 7.1 or later
- 16 MB of RAM memory (20 MB recommended)
- 20 MB of free hard disk space (30 MB recommended)
- 9" Powerbook or 12" or larger monitor
- High-density disk drive (CD-ROM recommended)

Instructional Package

The instructional package includes the student book, template disks, solutions disks, and teacher's manual.

The **student's book** is organized around the following features:

Objectives at the beginning of each lesson give students an overview of the lesson.

Concepts are explained in short, easy-to-understand segments with illustrations to serve as reference points.

Exercises immediately follow the presentation of new concepts. The instructions give students the opportunity to practice what they have just learned.

Review questions test for students' knowledge of concepts.

Review exercises check the students' understanding of the concepts and operations.

A **comprehensive index** provides quick and easy accessibility to specific parts of the book.

Template disks contain prekeyed text and selected graphics for exercises and review exercises and may be copied for students. These disks allow students to use class time learning desktop publishing rather than keying lengthy text into the computer.

Solutions disks contain solutions to exercises and review exercises so the teacher can check students' work.

The **teacher's manual** includes the following features to ensure a successful and an enjoyable teaching experience:

General teaching suggestions for effective instruction with a minimum of stress.

Specific teaching suggestions for each lesson.

An **answer key** for activities.

Solutions printouts for exercises and review exercises.

Acknowledgements

The author thanks Susan Lake, a teacher at Lubbock-Cooper High School, for her fine work in producing this book.

Many professional South-Western sales representatives make educationally sound presentations to teachers about our books. I have traveled with them "on the road," so I know first-hand and appreciate very much their valuable function as "bridges" between the author and teacher.

William R. Pasewark, Sr.

contents

contents

contents

Introducing PageMaker 6.0

❖ OBJECTIVES

Upon completion of this lesson, you will be able to:

1. Start PageMaker.
2. Create a new publication.
3. Identify parts of the publication window.
4. Close the publication window.
5. Open an existing publication.
6. Print a publication.
7. Save a publication.
8. End a PageMaker session.

Estimated Time: 1 hour

❖ INTRODUCTION

PageMaker is a popular desktop publishing program that gives you the power to create professional-looking documents such as brochures, newsletters, and reports. PageMaker is available in versions for the Macintosh and for computers using Windows. PageMaker generally uses the same instructions for both platforms. When the instructions are different, this text includes a set of instructions for Windows users and a set for Macintosh users.

❖ STARTING PAGEMAKER

PageMaker is opened from the Programs folder on the Start menu in Windows and from the desktop in Macintosh. Your instructor will help you find the location of the program.

To start PageMaker:

Windows

- Click the **Start** button on the taskbar**.**
- Highlight **Programs**.
- In the Programs menu, highlight **Adobe** by moving the mouse pointer to it. A submenu appears. Highlight **PageMaker 6.0** and then click.

note

Pressing and then quickly releasing the mouse button is called *clicking*. Clicking twice rapidly is called *double-clicking*. *Highlighting* an item on a menu requires moving the mouse pointer to the item. When the option is highlighted, the words appear in white letters in a dark box. Click once to execute the highlighted option.

Macintosh

- If the PageMaker 6.0 icon is on the desktop, double-click it.
- If the PageMaker 6.0 icon is not on the desktop, double-click the folder containing your applications, then the **Adobe PageMaker 6.0** folder, and then the **PageMaker 6.0** icon.

Start PageMaker.

1. Turn on your computer if necessary.
2. Select PageMaker:

   Windows
   a. Click the **Start** button on the taskbar**.**
   b. Select **Programs**.
   c. Click on **PageMaker 6.0**.

   Macintosh
   a. If the PageMaker 6.0 icon appears on the desktop, double-click it.
   b. If the PageMaker 6.0 icon is not on the desktop, double-click the **Applications** folder, then the **Adobe PageMaker 6.0** folder, and then the **PageMaker 6.0** icon.
3. Leave PageMaker open for the next exercise.

❖ CREATING A NEW PUBLICATION

After you start PageMaker, a blank screen appears with the PageMaker menu bar at the top. To access the options on a menu:

Windows

- Point to the menu name and click. A menu drops down, displaying the options available.
- Click the command you want to use.

Macintosh

- Point to the menu name. Press and hold down the mouse button. A menu drops down from the name, displaying the options available. The menu disappears if the mouse button is released.
- Drag the pointer down the menu and release the mouse button on the highlighted command you want to use.

You use the New command on the File menu to create a new PageMaker document, which is commonly referred to as a *publication*.

To create a new publication:

- Choose **New** on the File menu. The Document Setup dialog box appears as shown in Figure 1–1.

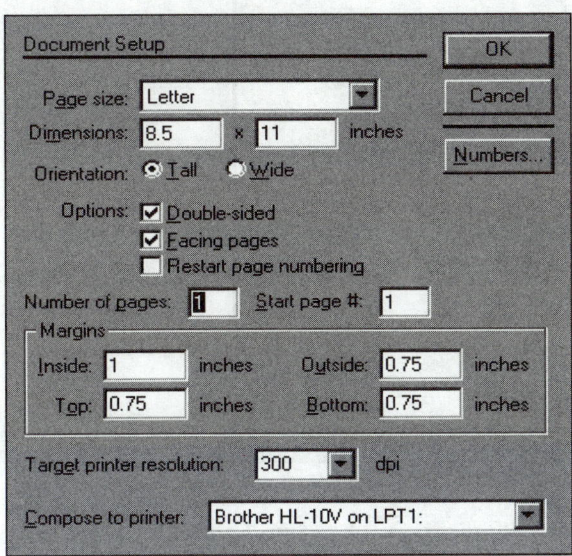

Figure 1–1 Document Setup dialog box with default settings. Windows (top); Macintosh (bottom)

- Click **OK** to accept the default settings. The *default* settings are those the computer automatically uses unless you specify otherwise. The same settings are present each time you open a new file. An empty page appears on the pasteboard, as shown in Figure 1–2. The *pasteboard* is the empty space surrounding the page where you can store text and graphics until you place them in a publication.

note

Default is the setting that the computer program automatically uses unless you make another choice.

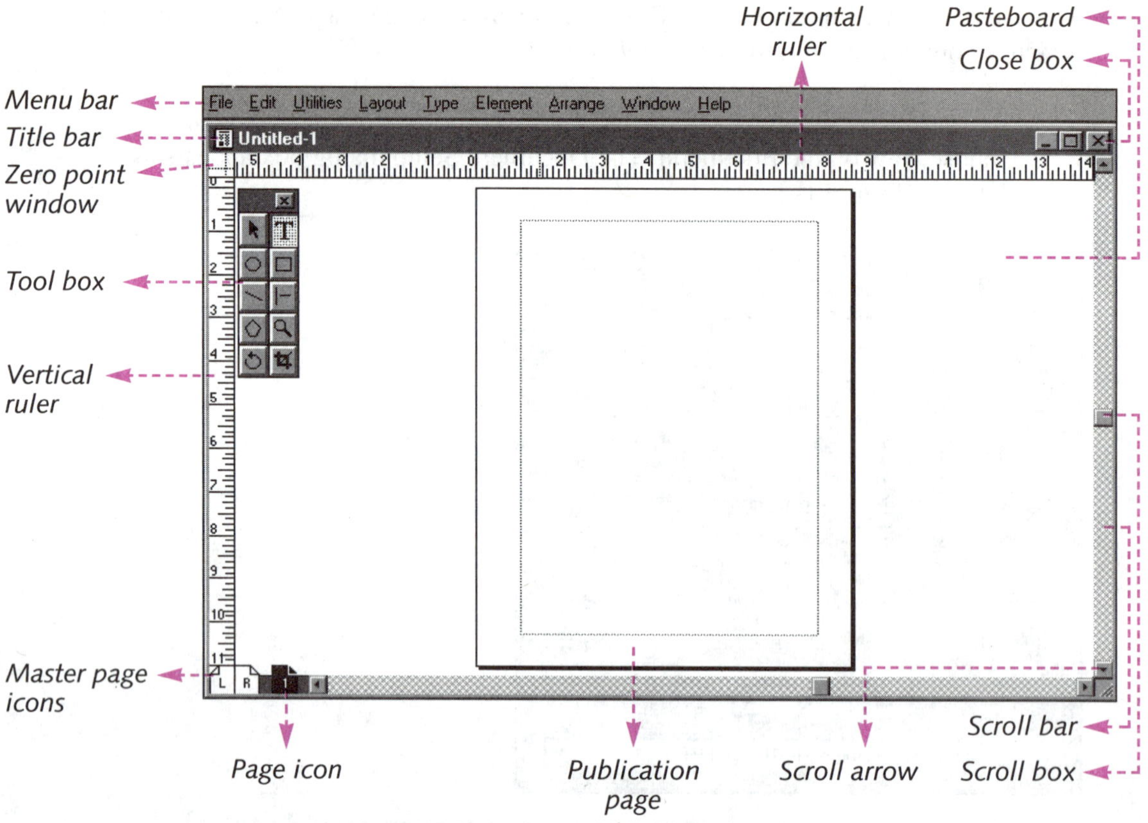

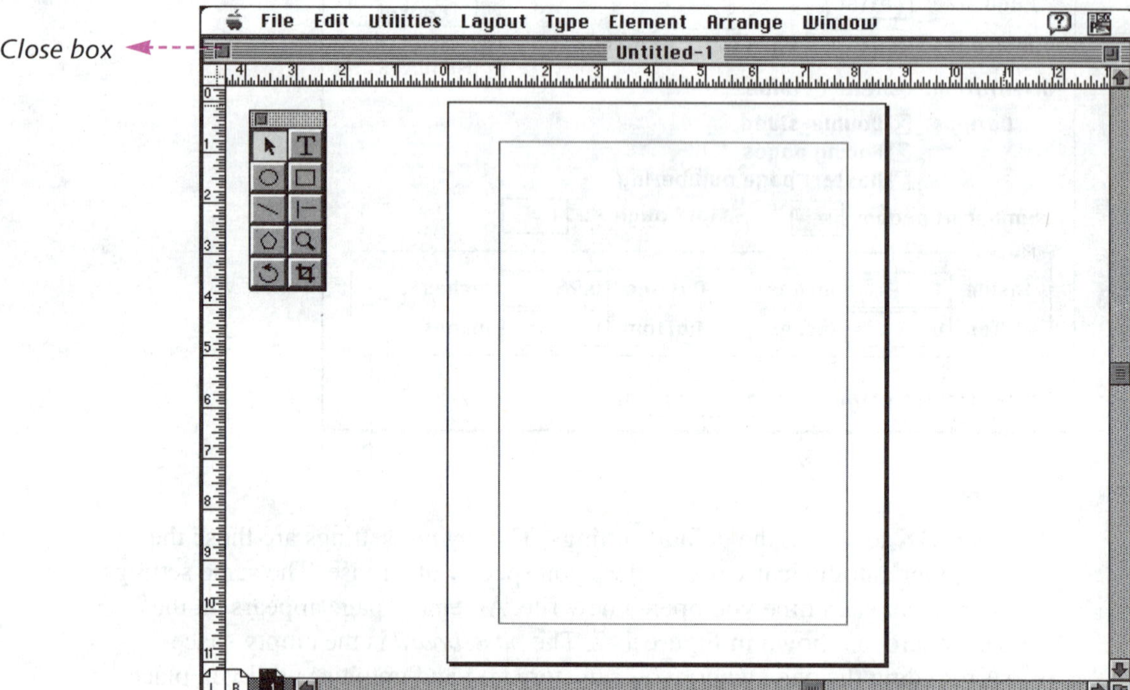

Figure 1–2 The publication window. Windows (top); Macintosh (bottom)

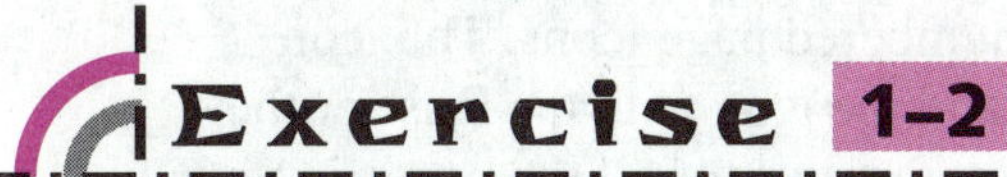

Exercise 1–2

Create a new publication.

1. Choose **New** on the File menu.
2. Click **OK** to accept the default settings in the Document Setup dialog box.
3. Leave the publication open for the next exercise.

> **note**
> Additional information on PageMaker is available in the on-line Help facility. If you are using Windows, click the Help menu to access help on a variety of topics. Macintosh users click the Guide menu in the upper right corner to access the Balloon Help feature.

❖ VIEWING THE PUBLICATION WINDOW

Notice the parts of the publication window labeled in Figure 1–2. They are explained below.

- The *menu bar* lists the names of the available program functions.
- The *title bar* shows the name of the publication you are viewing in the window. "Untitled" is the name assigned by PageMaker until you save the publication under a new file name.
- The *horizontal ruler* located at the top of the screen and the *vertical ruler* at the left side of the screen help you align text and graphics to specific measurements. The unit of measure shown is inches, but you can change it using the Preferences command on the File menu.
- The *close box* lets you close the window. Closing makes the window disappear from the screen but does not close the program. To close a PageMaker publication in Windows, click the "x" in the upper right corner of the publication page. In Macintosh, click the square in the upper left corner of the publication page.
- The *pasteboard* is the empty space around the page on the screen. You can place text and graphics in this area and move them onto your page later. Objects placed on the pasteboard will not print.
- When part of the publication is not visible on the screen, *scroll bars* appear. *Scroll arrows* and *scroll boxes* are located within scroll bars and are used to move the page vertically or horizontally. The scroll boxes indicate your approximate position on the publication page. Clicking on the scroll arrows moves the page a short distance. Click above or below the scroll box to move longer distances. You can also drag the scroll box to move to a specific part of a page. Scroll bars appear in places other than publication windows. In some dialog boxes, you see scroll bars on lists of files and directories.
- The *publication page* is a solid outline representing the actual page. Colored or dotted lines within the page indicate the page margins.
- A numbered *page icon* appears in the lower left corner of your screen. The icon for the page you are working on is darkened. In Figure 1–2, only one page is shown, and it is marked with a 1. If another page were added, you would see an icon marked with a 2 for the second page. To move to a specific page in a PageMaker publication, click on the desired page icon.

- The *master page icons* are to the left of the numbered page icons. The icon marked with an L is for the left master page and the icon with the R is for the right master page. The master pages serve as templates for all the pages in your publication. They contain formatting that is applied to corresponding pages, but they do not print.
- The *zero point* is the location on your page where the zeros on the horizontal and vertical rulers meet. When you start a new publication, the zero point is at the upper left corner of the page. You can move the zero point anywhere along the ruler by dragging a zero point marker to a new location. The markers are vertical and horizontal dotted lines located in the zero point window.
- The *Toolbox*, shown in Figure 1–3, contains tools used to create and modify text and graphics and to change the viewable area. To select a tool, point and click on it. Table 1–1 lists the tools and their functions.

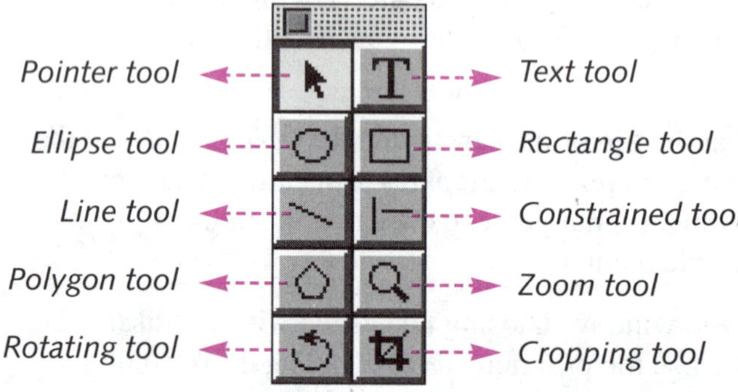

Figure 1–3 The Toolbox provides tools for manipulating text and graphics.

Table 1–1 Tool functions

Tool	Use It To
Pointer tool	Select and move text and graphics
Text tool	Select and key text
Rectangle tool	Draw rectangles and squares
Constrained tool	Draw straight lines at 45-degree angles
Zoom tool	Magnify or reduce the viewing area
Cropping tool	Crop imported graphics
Rotating tool	Rotate text blocks and graphics
Polygon tool	Draw multisided objects
Line tool	Draw straight lines
Ellipse tool	Draw ovals and circles

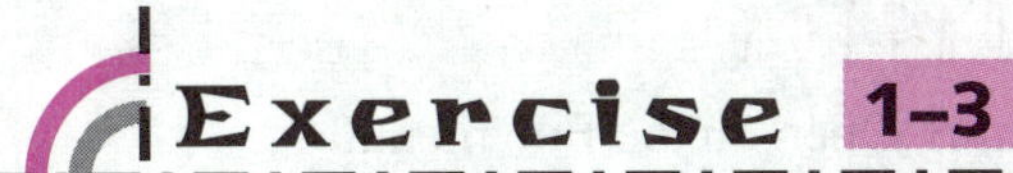

Exercise 1-3

Move around the publication window.

1. Click the **Edit** menu. If you are using Windows, click anywhere on the screen to close the menu. Macintosh users simply release the mouse button.
2. Click the **Utilities** menu, and then close the menu.
3. Click the right-pointing scroll arrow to move the publication horizontally.
4. Click the down-pointing scroll arrow to move the publication vertically.
5. Leave the publication open for the next exercise.

note

When you pull down a menu, notice the symbols to the right of some menu selections. These are keyboard shortcuts allowing you to execute commands without using the mouse. Shortcuts require you to press either the Ctrl key (Windows) or the Command key (Macintosh) plus a letter. Learning to use these shortcuts can speed up your use of the program.

❖ CLOSING A PUBLICATION

Closing a publication removes the publication from the screen. If you have made any unsaved changes to the publication, a dialog box like the one shown in Figure 1–4 displays, asking if you want to save the changes to your publication before closing. If you want to save the changes, choose Yes. If you do not want to save the changes, choose No. If you decide not to close the publication, choose Cancel.

To close a publication:

- Choose **Close** on the **File** menu.

  or
- Click the **Close** box.

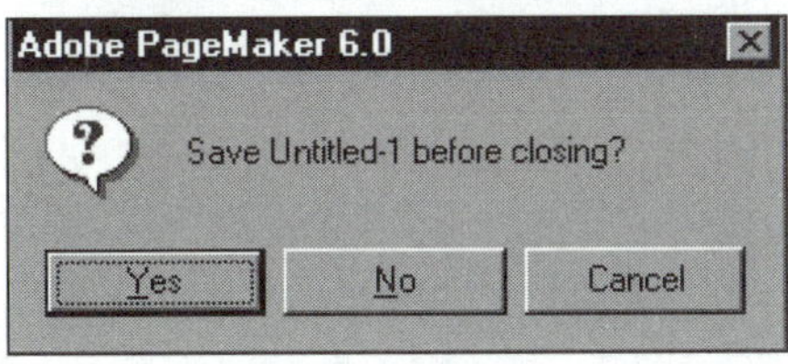

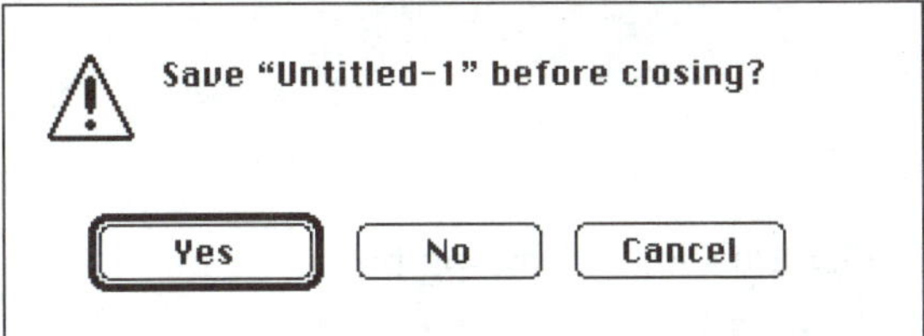

Figure 1–4
The Save message box appears to warn you about modifications made in a publication. Windows (top); Macintosh (bottom)

Exercise 1-4

Close a PageMaker publication.

1. Choose **Close** on the **File** menu. If a dialog box appears asking if you want to save changes, click **No**. The blank page disappears.
2. Leave the screen as is for the next exercise.

note

Files are individual documents created with programs such as PageMaker. Folders contain files and other folders.

❖ OPENING AN EXISTING PUBLICATION

You can open an existing PageMaker file by selecting Open on the File menu. The Open Publication dialog box appears, similar to that shown in Figure 1–5. A PageMaker file can be opened from a disk, your computer's hard drive, a network, or another storage device. Your instructor will show you where to find the template files you will use to complete the exercises in this tutorial.

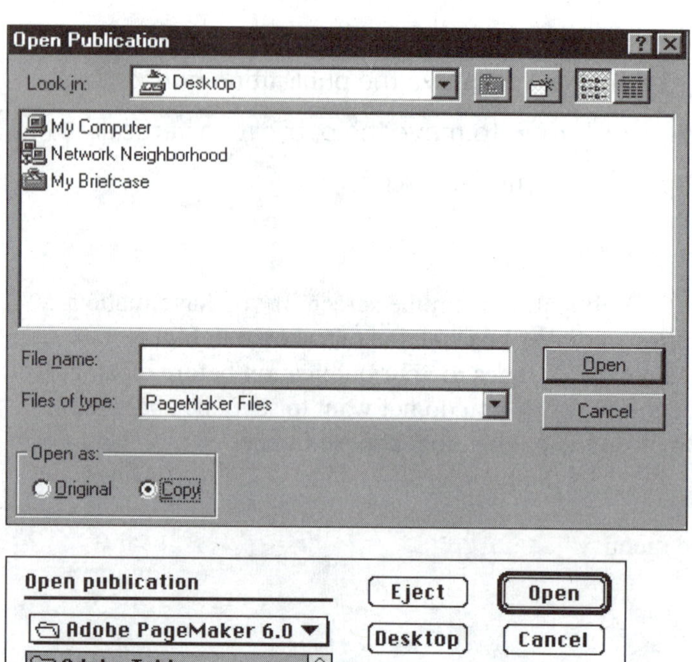

Figure 1–5
You open PageMaker files by selecting them in the Open Publication dialog box. Windows (top); Macintosh (bottom)

To open a publication:

Windows

- Choose **Open** on the File menu. The Open Publication dialog box appears.
- In the Look in box, click on the arrow to display a list of choices.
- Click the name of the disk that contains the file you want to open.
- If the publication is in a folder on the disk, double-click on the folder name. This step can be repeated as often as needed to reach the desired file.
- Double-click the name of the publication to open it, or highlight the name of the publication. The filename appears in the File Name box. Click **Open**.

Macintosh

- Choose **Open** on the File menu. The Open publication dialog box appears.
- Click the button labeled **Desktop**.

- Double-click the name of the disk or drive that contains the file.
- If the publication is in a folder on the disk, double-click on the folder name. This step can be repeated as often as needed to reach the desired file.
- Double-click the name of the publication, or highlight the name of the publication and then click **Open** or **OK**.

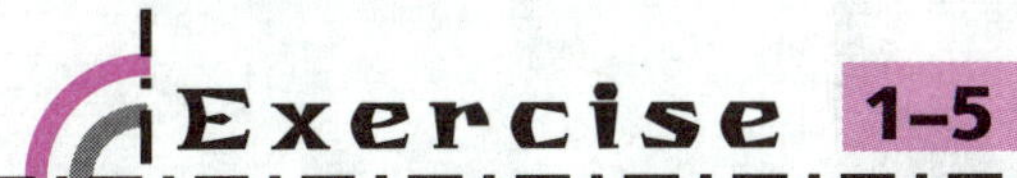

Open an existing publication.

1. Choose **Open** on the File menu.
2. From the template files accompanying this course, open the publication **Define**. (Your instructor will tell you how to access the template files.)
3. Leave the publication open for the next exercise.

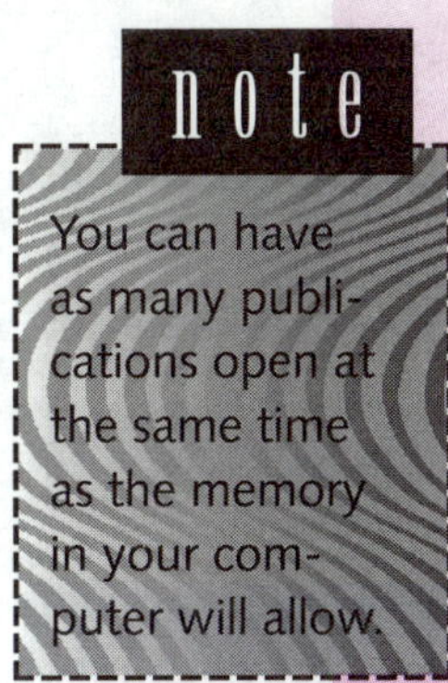

SAVING YOUR WORK

Saving is one of the most important features of any computer program. You can save files to a floppy disk or to the hard drive of a computer.

You save a publication by using the Save or Save As commands on the File menu. The first time you save a publication, choose Save on the File menu. The Save Publication dialog box appears like that shown in Figure 1–6.

The dialog box indicates that the file is untitled. Key a name for the file in the file name box. Select the drive and/or folder to which you want to save the file.

The next time you want to save your publication, choose Save on the File menu. Since the publication has already been saved with a file name, no dialog box appears. PageMaker saves the current publication by overwriting the previous version of it.

If you want to save your file under a new name or to a new location, choose Save As on the File menu. The Save Publication dialog box appears. Key in a new name or select a new location. The new file is saved to the new location. The original publication remains unchanged.

To save a publication for the first time:

- Choose **Save** on the File menu. The Save Publication dialog box appears.

Windows

- In the Save in box, click the arrow to drop down a list of choices.
- Click on the name of the drive and/or folder to which you want to save the file.
- Delete the word *Untitled* in the File Name *box* and key the new name of your publication.
- Click **Save**. The dialog box closes and you are returned to your publication.

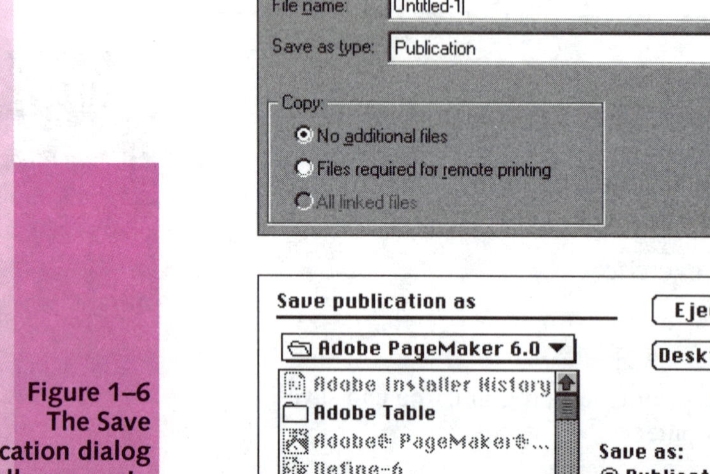

Figure 1–6 The Save Publication dialog box allows you to save a file with a specific name and to a specific location. Windows (top); Macintosh (bottom)

Macintosh

- Click **Desktop**.
- Double-click the name of the drive and/or folder to which you want to save the file.
- Delete the word *Untitled* and key the new name of your publication.
- Click **OK**. The dialog box closes and you are returned to your publication.

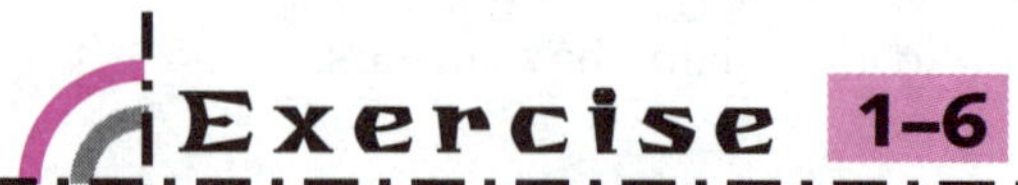

Exercise 1–6

Save a publication.

1. Rename the **Define** publication by saving it with a new filename:

   Windows

   a. Choose **Save As** on the File menu. In the Save in box, click the arrow to drop down a list of choices.
   b. Click the drive and/or folder to which you want to save the file. (Your instructor will tell you where to save your course files.)

c. Delete the word *Define* in the File name box and enter **Ex1-6**.
d. Click **Save**.

Macintosh

a. Choose **Save as** on the File menu. Click **Desktop**.
b. Double-click the name of the drive and/or folder to which you want to save the file. (Your instructor will tell you where to save your course files.)
c. Highlight the word *Define* in the file name box and enter **Ex1-6**.
d. Click **OK**.

2. Leave the publication open for the next exercise.

❖ PRINTING A PUBLICATION

The Print command on the File menu lets you produce a publication on paper. You can determine the number of copies to print, which pages to print, and the orientation of the paper. You will learn more about printing options in a later lesson.

To print a publication:

- Choose **Print** on the File menu. The Print Document dialog box appears as shown in Figure 1–7.
- Click **Print**.

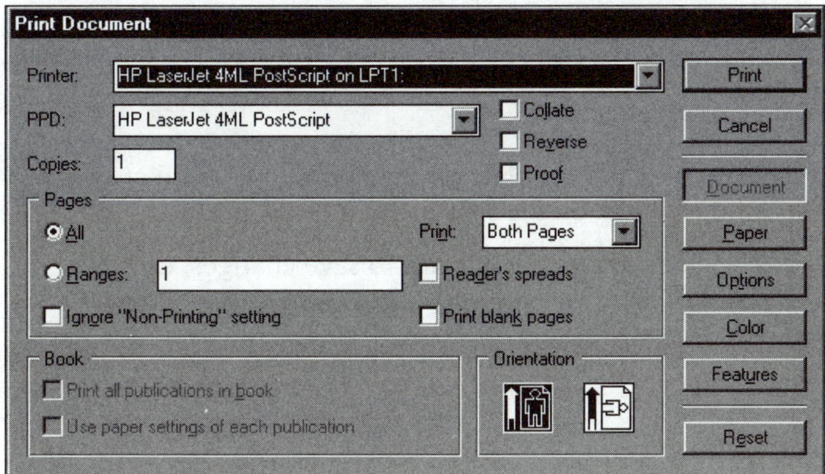

Figure 1-7 The Print Document dialog box. Windows (top); Macintosh (bottom)

Print a publication.

1. Choose **Print** on the File menu.
2. Select a printer, if necessary. Leave the other settings as they are. Click **Print**.
3. Leave the publication open for the next exercise.

❖ ENDING A PAGEMAKER SESSION

It is important to end your PageMaker session whenever you leave your computer. This ensures that your work is saved and that the computer is ready for the next user.

End your PageMaker session by choosing Exit (Windows) or Quit (Macintosh) on the File menu. If you have not saved a publication, you are prompted to save it at this time. The PageMaker program closes, and you are returned to the Windows or the Macintosh desktop.

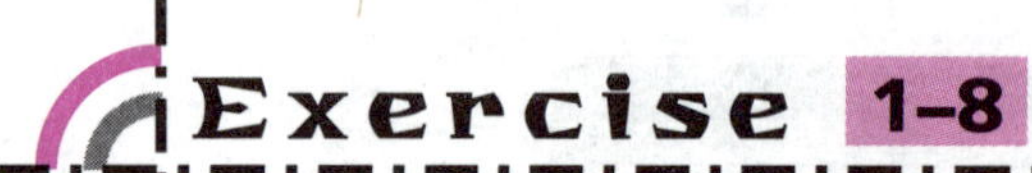

End a PageMaker session.

1. If you are using Windows, choose **Exit** on the File menu. If you are a Macintosh user, choose **Quit** on the **File** menu.
2. If a message box appears asking if you want to save changes, click **No.**

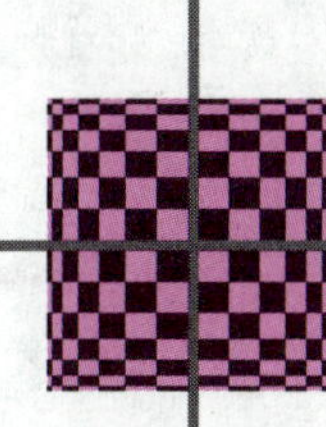

activities

❖ TRUE/FALSE

On the blank line before each sentence, place a **T** *if the statement is true and an* **F** *if it is false.*

____ 1. When you start PageMaker, a new publication opens automatically.

____ 2. Scroll bars are used to view parts of the publication not visible on the screen.

____ 3. Closing a publication erases your file.

____ 4. To end your PageMaker session, choose Stop on the File menu.

____ 5. You can choose Save As to give your existing file a different name or to save it to a new location.

❖ COMPLETION

Answer the questions below in the space provided.

6. How do you move to a specific page in a PageMaker publication?

____

____

7. On what part of the screen can you place text and then later move it onto a page?

____

____

8. What are four tools from the toolbox and their functions?

____

____

9. What are two ways to close a publication?

____

____

10. If a publication has already been saved for the first time, what will choosing the Save command do?

____

____

review

Review Exercise 1-1

Open, print, and close a file in PageMaker.

1. Start PageMaker if necessary.
2. Choose **Open** on the File menu.
3. From the template files accompanying this course, open **Fun**.
4. Save the publication as **Re1-1** to the folder or disk indicated by your instructor.
5. Print the publication.
6. Close the publication without saving changes, and end your PageMaker session.

Working with Text

❖ OBJECTIVES

Upon completion of this lesson, you will be able to:

1. Change the view of a PageMaker publication.
2. Enter text.
3. Highlight text.
4. Delete, cut, copy, and paste text.
5. Import text.
6. Change the size of a text block.
7. Move a text block.
8. Delete, cut, copy, and paste a text block.
9. Link text blocks.

Estimated Time: 1 hour

❖ CHANGING THE VIEW

PageMaker allows you to look at publications on the screen in many different views. New publications on your screen are shown in Fit in Window view. You can also view publications at their actual size and at 25%, 50%, 75%, 200%, and 400% of actual size. You can show the whole pasteboard using the Entire Pasteboard command on the View submenu on the Layout menu. Changing the view to see the entire pasteboard is helpful when you want to work with the overall layout. When you are working on specific text or graphics, you will want a closer view.

To change the view of a publication:

- Choose **View** on the Layout menu. A submenu appears, as shown in Figure 2–1.
- Click on the view you want.

You can also use the Zoom tool in the toolbox to change the page view. The Zoom tool lets you move quickly between preset magnifications. When you select the Zoom tool, the pointer becomes a magnifying glass icon containing a plus sign. This indicates that when you click on a portion of the page, the view is enlarged. You can reduce the view by holding down the Ctrl key (Windows) or the Option key (Macintosh) as you click on portions of the page. When you reduce the view, a minus sign appears in the icon.

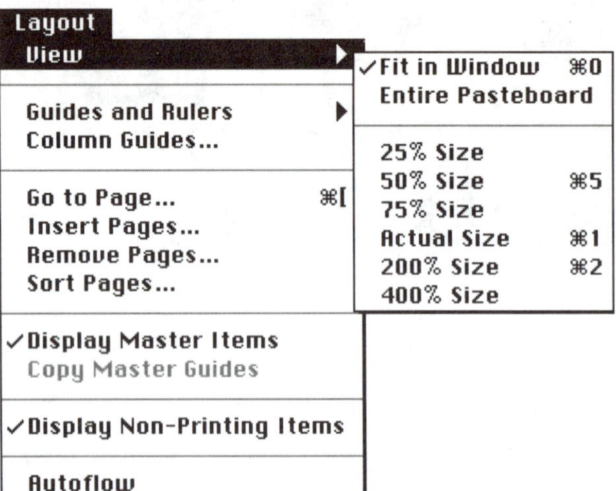

Figure 2–1
Change your view to fit your desktop publishing needs.

You can select a specific area to be enlarged or reduced by dragging the Zoom tool so that it "boxes" the area you want to view. "Boxing" a portion of the publication is the only way you can enlarge the view of your publication to 800%.

Exercise 2–1

Change the view of the publication.

1. Open **Ex1-6** from the folder or disk containing your course files.
2. Maximize the publication window by clicking the maximize button in the upper right corner. In Windows, it is the box to the left of the "X." In Macintosh, it is the double box.
3. Select **View** on the Layout menu, and then select **Actual Size**.
4. Select **View** on the Layout menu again, and then select **200% Size**.
5. Change the view to **Fit in Window**.
6. Select the **Zoom** tool. Click twice on the text in the center of the page to enlarge it to 75%.
7. Continue clicking three more times to enlarge it to 200%.
8. Hold down the **Ctrl** key (Windows) or the **Option** key (Macintosh) and click until the publication fits in the window again.
9. Close the publication by selecting **Close** on the File menu. Do not save changes.

❖ ENTERING TEXT

The Text tool in the Toolbox is used to key text in PageMaker. When you select the Text tool, it becomes an *I-beam*. When you click on the page where you want to enter text, the I-beam changes to a blinking vertical line called a *cursor*. You begin keying text at this *insertion point*. Text is contained in a *text block*. A page can contain numerous text blocks. You begin a new text block by clicking on the page with the Text tool.

The top and bottom borders of a text block have *handles* in the middle. You can drag these handles up and down to change the depth of the text block. That is why they are often referred to as *windowshades*. (See Figure 2–2.) You can change the depth and width of a text block by dragging one of the small squares, also called *handles*, at the end of each border. You can see the border only when a text block is selected.

To select a text block, click on the text with the pointer tool. To deselect a text block, click outside the text block.

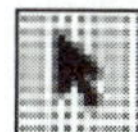

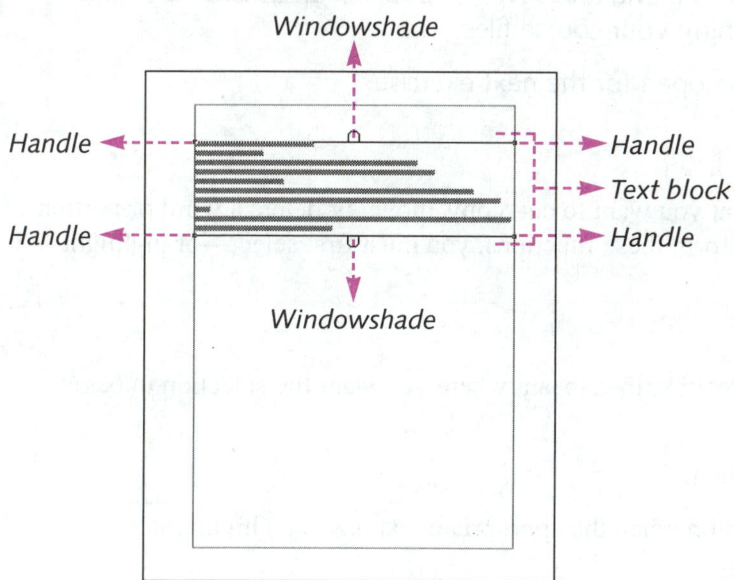

Figure 2–2
The upper and lower borders of a text block can be rolled up or down like windowshades.

Exercise 2–2

Key text in a publication.

1. Create a new publication by selecting **New** on the File menu. Click **OK** in the Document Setup box.
2. Change the view of the publication to **Actual Size**. Scroll so you can see the top left corner of the page.
3. Enter a heading at the top of the page that identifies your work:
   a. Select the Text tool.
   b. Click the I-beam at a point above the top margin line but still within the page.
   c. Key in a heading—your instructor will tell you information to be included.
4. Click the I-beam in the upper left corner of the page within the page margins.
5. Key the following text:

note

The Toolbox and other "floating" palettes can be moved to other locations if they cover the area in which you need to work. With the pointer tool, click the title bar at the top of the toolbox or palette and drag it to a new location.

```
The main objectives of a layout are readability and visual appeal.
Enliven a publication with graphics that relate to the text. A
publication with a well-designed page layout can motivate the reader
and keep their interest.
```

6. Select **Save** on the File menu and save the publication as **Ex2-2** to the folder or disk containing your course files.
7. Leave the publication open for the next exercise.

❖ HIGHLIGHTING TEXT

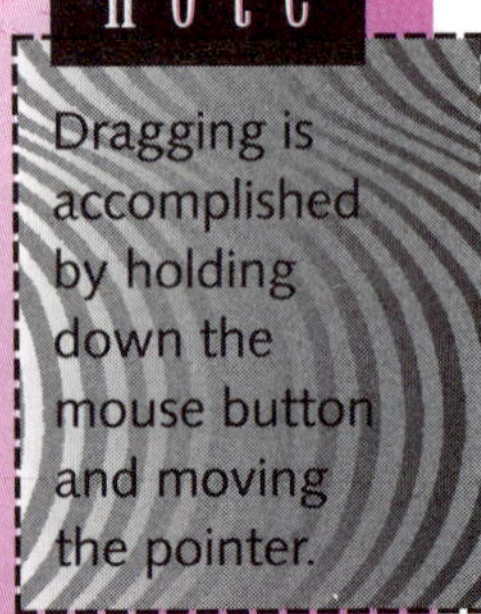

Dragging is accomplished by holding down the mouse button and moving the pointer.

Frequently, you will find that you want to cut, copy, move, or delete a word or portion of the text you enter. To perform these functions, you must first select—or highlight—the text.

To highlight text:

- Select the Text tool. Position the I-beam where you want the selection to begin and click.
- Drag to highlight the text.
- Release the mouse button when the appropriate text has been highlighted.

Exercise 2-3

Highlight text.

1. If necessary, select the **Text** tool. Click in front of the word *readability* in the first line and drag the I-beam across it.
2. Remove the highlighting by clicking outside the highlighted word.
3. Highlight the words *well-designed*. Deselect them.
4. Leave the publication open for the next exercise.

❖ DELETING, CUTTING, COPYING, AND PASTING TEXT

Once text is selected, you can manipulate it in a variety of ways. You can delete it, or you can copy or move it to another location by using the Cut, Copy, and Paste commands on the Edit menu. (See Figure 2–3.) To delete selected text, press the Backspace or Delete keys.

To copy selected text and paste it to another location, choose Copy on the Edit menu. The text is placed in a temporary storage area called the *Clipboard*. Position the cursor in the location where you want the copied text to appear, and then select Paste on the Edit menu.

Edit
Cannot Undo ⌘Z
Cut ⌘X
Copy ⌘C
Paste ⌘V
Clear
Multiple Paste...
Select All ⌘A
Editions ▶
Paste Special...
Insert Object...
Edit Story ⌘E
Edit Original

Figure 2–3
The Cut, Copy, and Paste commands allow you to move text from one place to another in a publication.

To move selected text from one location to another, choose Cut on the Edit menu. The text is removed from the original location and placed on the Clipboard. Position the cursor in the new location, and then select Paste on the Edit menu to move the text.

note

If you accidentally delete, cut, or paste text, you can reverse the action by using the Undo command on the Edit menu. This command can undo only the most recent command or action.

Exercise 2-4

Cut and copy text.

1. Position the I-beam before the word *their* in the last sentence of the text. Click and drag until it and the space following it are highlighted.
2. Press **Delete** or **Backspace**.
3. Place the cursor before the word *interest*. Key **his or her**. Press the **spacebar**.
4. Highlight the second sentence including the space after the period.
5. Select **Cut** on the Edit menu.
6. Position the cursor after the period at the end of the paragraph.
7. Press **Enter** twice to create a blank line between the paragraphs.
8. Select **Paste** on the Edit menu.
9. Save the publication as **Ex2-4**.
10. Leave the publication open for the next exercise.

note

The Revert command on the File menu is similar to Undo. Revert allows you to return to the last saved version of the publication; however, changes you have not saved are lost.

❖ IMPORTING TEXT

In creating publications, you will find that you frequently want to place text that's already been entered in another program file. For example, you might have a form letter created in a word processing program that you want to place in a publication so you can add graphics and different formatting. PageMaker supports a variety of word processing programs.

To place text:

- Choose **Place** on the File menu. The Place Document dialog box appears like that shown in Figure 2–4. Choose the file you want to place.

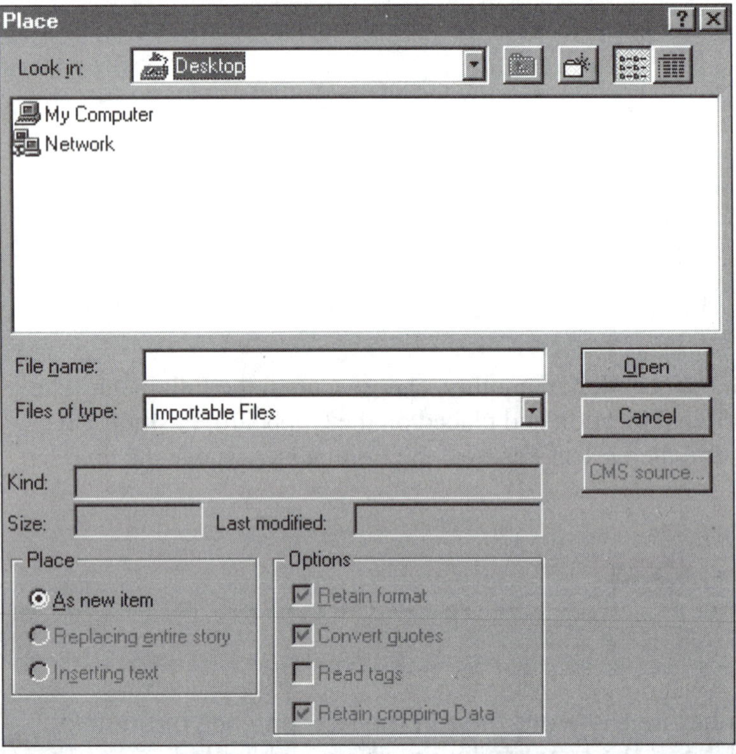

Figure 2–4
Select a file to place from the Place Document dialog box. Windows (top); Macintosh (bottom)

- Select a Place option. You can place the file as a new item or story, replace an existing story with the new file, or insert the file into an existing story. A *story* is a complete text file that can be contained in one or several text blocks. You will learn more about stories in the next lesson.
- Click **Open** (Windows) or **OK** (Macintosh).

- A Text-only import filter dialog box like that shown in Figure 2–5 might appear. This dialog box appears when a file with a .txt extension (indicating a text formatted file) is being placed. Click **OK**.

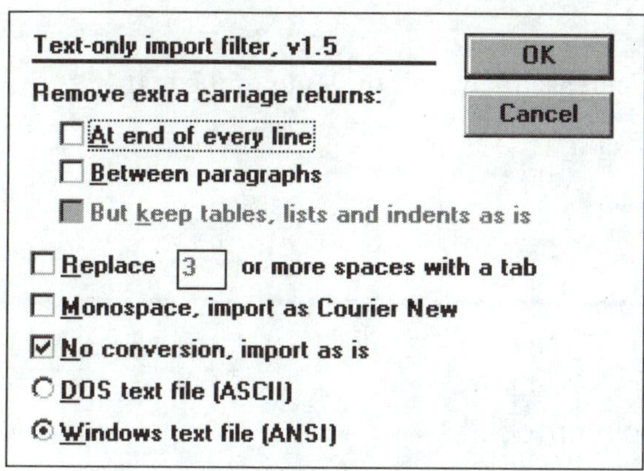

Figure 2–5
Text-only import filter dialog box

- Depending on the Place option you selected, the text is either automatically inserted into the existing text at the location where you've positioned the cursor. Or, if you selected the option to place the text as a new story, the pointer appears on the page as a "loaded cursor." Click where you want the text to begin. The text is "released" and placed on the page.

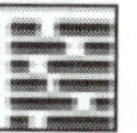

Place text in a publication.

1. If necessary, place the cursor at the end of the last sentence and press the **spacebar**.
2. Choose **Place** on the File menu.
3. In the Place dialog box, select the file **Obj** from the template files accompanying this course. From the Place options, select the **Inserting text** option.
4. Click **Open** (Windows) or **OK** (Macintosh).
5. Click **OK** in the Text-only import filter dialog box. The text is inserted at the end of the text.
6. Save the publication as **Ex2-5** to the folder or disk containing your course files.
7. Leave the publication open for the next exercise.

CHANGING THE SIZE OF A TEXT BLOCK

As you learned earlier, text is contained in a text block. Text blocks can be enlarged or reduced using the handles and windowshades.

To change the depth and width of a text block:

- Select the text block.
- Place the pointer on a corner handle and hold down the mouse button until the pointer becomes a two-sided arrow.
- Drag in any direction to increase or decrease the width or depth of the text block.

Exercise 2-6

Change the size of a text block.

1. Click on the text block with the pointer tool.
2. In the **Layout** menu, select **View**. Change the view to **Fit in Window**.
3. Click the top right handle of the text block and drag it to the left until the size of the text block is 3 inches wide. Use the ruler at the top of the page as a guide. (Note that the text block starts at the 1-inch mark.)
4. Click on the bottom left handle. Drag the handle down to about the 5-inch mark to make the text block longer.
5. Save the publication as **Ex2-6**.
6. Leave the publication open for the next exercise.

❖ MOVING A TEXT BLOCK

Just as you can change the size of a text block, you can easily move text blocks.

To move a text block:

- Select the text block.
- Place the pointer anywhere on the text block.
- Press and hold down the mouse button until the pointer becomes a four-sided arrow.
- Drag the text block to the new location. Release the mouse button.

Exercise 2-7

Move a text block.

1. Select the text block and drag it to the lower right corner of the page.
2. Save the publication as **Ex2-7**.
3. Leave the publication open for the next exercise.

❖ DELETING, CUTTING, COPYING, AND PASTING A TEXT BLOCK

Just as you can manipulate individual words and portions of text, you can delete, cut, copy, and paste an entire text block. To delete a selected text block, press the Backspace or Delete keys.

To copy a selected text block and paste it to a new location, choose Copy on the Edit menu. A copy of the text block is placed on the Clipboard. Choose Paste on the Edit menu. A copy of the text block appears overlapping the original. Click on the text block and drag it to the new location. Or you can select the Text tool and position the I-beam at the location where you want the copied text to appear. Then select Paste on the Edit menu.

To remove a selected text block from its original location and move it to a new location, follow the steps above except select Cut from the Edit menu instead of Copy.

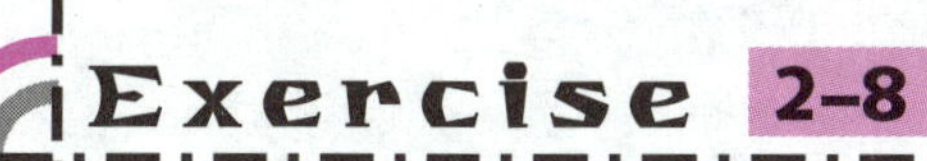

Cut and copy text blocks.

1. Select the text block and then choose **Copy** on the Edit menu.
2. Select **Paste** on the Edit menu.
3. Drag the selected text block to the top left corner of the page.
4. Drag the bottom right handle of the top text block up and to the right margin.
5. Select the text block at the bottom of the page and press **Delete** or **Backspace**.
6. Select the **Undo Clear** (Windows) or **Undo Delete** (Macintosh) command on the Edit menu. The text block reappears.
7. Save the publication as **Ex2-8**.
8. Leave the publication open for the next exercise.

❖ LINKING TEXT BLOCKS

You might have noticed when you were adjusting the size of the text block that an arrow appeared in the lower windowshade handle. This means that the text block contains more text that currently is not visible. You can drag the handle down to reveal the text. Or you can click on the arrow in the windowshade handle to "load" the cursor with the remaining text. Click elsewhere in the publication to place the text as a new text block.

A plus sign in the windowshade handle indicates that the text is continued in another text block. After all text has been placed in one text block or a series of text blocks, an empty windowshade handle appears at the end of the story. (See Figure 2–6).

If the first text block is enlarged to reveal more text, text in any subsequent blocks reflect the change.

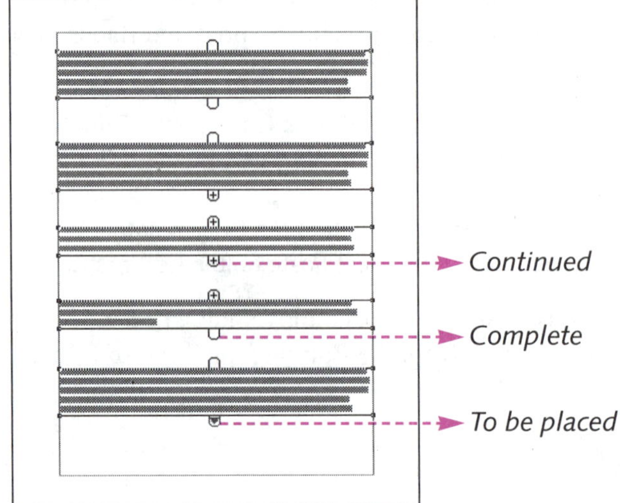

Figure 2–6 Windowshade handles indicate whether the story in the text block is complete, continued, or needs to be placed.

Exercise 2–9

Manipulate text blocks.

1. Select the bottom text block and drag the bottom windowshade up so that only the first paragraph is visible. Notice that an arrow appears in the windowshade handle.
2. Click on the triangle. The pointer changes to a loaded cursor.
3. Click below the existing text block to release the text. Drag the new text block to the bottom of the page.
4. Go back to the first paragraph and select it. Drag the bottom windowshade down so the entire second paragraph is visible. Notice the change in the bottom text block.
5. Save the publication as **Ex2-9**.
6. Print the publication by selecting **Print** on the File menu. Then click **Print** in the Print Document dialog box.
7. Close the publication and select **Yes** in the save message box. End your PageMaker session.

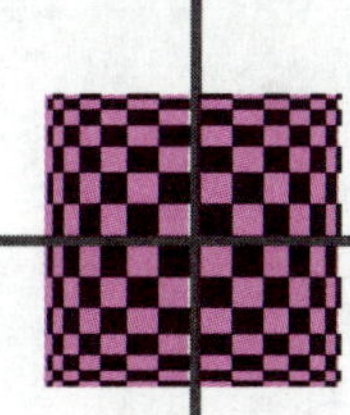

activities

❖ TRUE/FALSE

*On the blank line before each sentence, place a **T** if the statement is true and an **F** if it is false.*

____ 1. A plus (+) symbol in the lower windowshade handle means that the rest of the story needs to be placed.

____ 2. Highlighting text is also called selecting text.

____ 3. The Edit and Paste commands are used to move text from one location to another.

____ 4. The Copy command removes the original text from the publication.

____ 5. The Undo command can undo only your last command or action.

❖ COMPLETION

Answer the questions below in the space provided.

6. Why would you want to change the view of a publication?

____

____

7. How do you delete an entire sentence from a text block?

____

____

8. What is the process for inserting a word in the middle of a paragraph?

____

____

9. How is text imported from a word processing program?

____

____

10. How do you change the size of a text block?

____

____

review

Review Exercise 2-1

Add and manipulate text in a publication.

1. From the template files, open the publication **Puppies**.
2. If necessary, maximize the window. Key your heading in the top margin.
3. Select the text block.
4. Drag the bottom windowshade handle down until all the text is showing.
5. Change the view to **Actual Size**.
6. Key **cute,** after *These*. (Be sure to leave one space between the comma and the word *healthy*.)
7. Key **915-** before *555* in the telephone number.
8. Highlight the two sentences that begin *These cute* and then select **Cut** on the Edit menu.
9. Place the cursor to the right of the 2 in the phone number and press **Enter** two times to create a blank line. Select **Paste** on the Edit menu.
10. Delete one blank line before *Call Rich*.
11. Copy the phone number and paste it at the bottom of the page. A new text block will be created. Drag it in place so that it rests in the center of the page on the bottom margin line.
12. Key **Call** before the phone number at the bottom of the page.
13. Delete the line *Free to Good Homes!*
14. Undo the Delete command. Deselect the text.
15. Change the view to **Fit in Window**.
16. Save the publication as **Re2-1**.
17. Print the publication and end your PageMaker session.

Using the Story Editor

❖ OBJECTIVES

Upon completion of this lesson, you will be able to:

1. Open the Story Editor window.
2. Create and place a story using the Story Editor.
3. Check spelling.
4. Find and change text.

Estimated Time: 1 hour

❖ OPENING THE STORY EDITOR

So far you have been working in PageMaker's Layout window, which lets you easily place and arrange objects on the page. Although you can also do basic word processing and editing functions in the Layout window, you will use the *Story Editor* to enter and edit most text.

As you learned in the last lesson, a story is a complete text file that can be contained in one or several text blocks. The Story Editor acts like a separate word processing program within the PageMaker program. It makes it possible to key text quickly, check for spelling errors, and see text without the distraction of other layout features.

To open the Story Editor, select Edit Story on the Edit menu. Text is displayed in the Story Editor in a single font and size, similar to that shown in Figure 3–1.

The Layout window moves to the back when the Story Editor window is opened. You can make the Layout window the active window by selecting it on the Window menu and then clicking Layout on the submenu. Or, if it is visible behind the Story Editor window, just click on it to make it active. Unless you close the Story Editor window, it will move to the back when you select the Layout window.

To edit a story that's already entered in a text block:

- Click anywhere in the text block with the **Text** tool, or select the text block with the pointer tool.
- Choose **Edit Story** on the Edit menu. The Story Editor window appears displaying the story.
- To return to the Layout window, close the Story Editor by clicking its **Close** box. If you want to leave the Story Editor open, choose the name of the publication on the Window menu and then select **Layout**, or if the Layout window is visible, click it to make it active.

note

The Preferences command on the File menu lets you customize the way you view your publication in the Story Editor. In the Preferences dialog box, choose More to get the More Preferences dialog box, which lets you change how text is displayed.

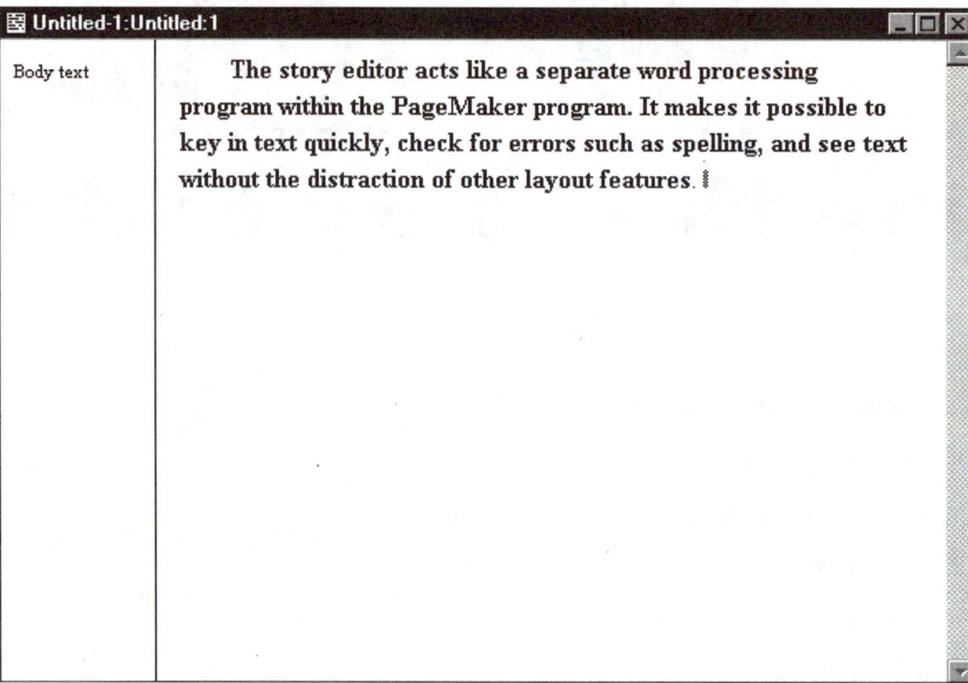

Figure 3–1
The Story Editor shows text set in a standard size and font. If you change the size, it is not apparent until you return to the Layout window.

To create a new story in the Story Editor:

- In the Layout window, make sure no text block is selected.
- Choose **Edit Story** on the Edit menu.
- Key the story.

Once you've created a new story, you can place it in your publication:

- Click the Story Editor **Close** box. The Place dialog box appears as shown in Figure 3–2. Click **Place.**
- When you are returned to the Layout window, a loaded cursor appears.
- Click the cursor where you want to locate the text.

Figure 3–2
The Place dialog box prompts you to place the new story in your PageMaker publication.

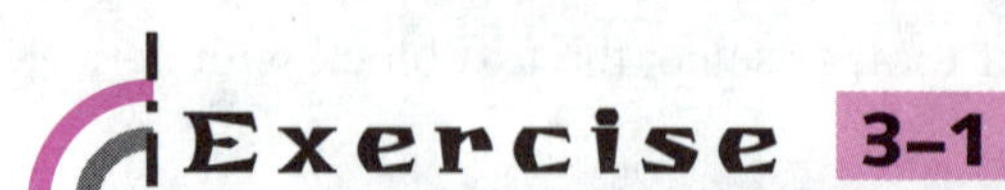

Open the Story Editor and create a new story.

1. From the template files, open **History**.
2. Maximize the window and change the view if necessary. Select the **Text** tool and key your heading in the top margin.

3. Choose **Edit Story** on the Edit menu. Your heading appears in the Story Editor, where you can edit it.
4. Choose **History** on the Window menu. Select **Layout**.
5. Change the view to **Fit in Window**. Click on an empty part of the publication page. Choose **Edit Story** on the Edit menu.
6. Key **History of Computers** in the Story Editor window. Close the story by clicking the **Close** box.
7. In the dialog box, select **Place**.
8. Position the loaded cursor above the large text block and click.
9. Save the publication as **Ex3-1** to the folder or disk containing your course files and leave it open for the next exercise.

❖ USING STORY EDITOR UTILITIES

In Story Editor you can check spelling and find and change characters, words, and phrases. These editing features are on the Utilities menu of the Story Editor.

USING THE SPELL CHECKER

PageMaker checks the spelling of words in your publication against its built-in dictionary. When it finds a word that is not in its dictionary, a possible capitalization error, or a double word error, you can replace it with a word suggested by PageMaker, enter a correction yourself, or ignore it. You also can add words to the dictionary.

To check spelling:

- In Story editor, choose **Spelling** on the Utilities menu. The Spelling dialog box appears, like the one shown in Figure 3–3. You can select from options to check spelling in selected text only, in one story in a publication, in all stories in a publication, or in all stories in all open publications. If you have highlighted text, the Selected text option will be available. If no text is highlighted, then only the Current story or All stories options are available.
- Click **Start**.
- When PageMaker finds a word it doesn't recognize, it displays it in the Change to text box. Click **Ignore** to continue without making a change, or choose a

note

Once you have chosen to ignore the spelling of a misspelled word, PageMaker continues to ignore that word until you close PageMaker. If you check your spelling a second time without closing PageMaker first, PageMaker will indicate that there are no spelling errors.

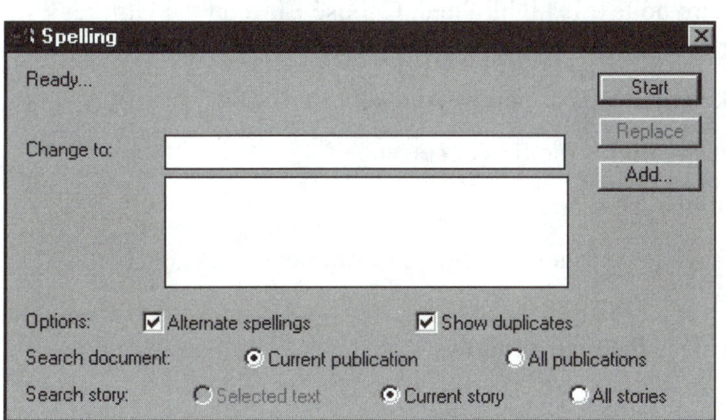

Figure 3–3
The Spelling dialog box allows you to check the spelling of words, ignore words, change misspelled words, or add words to the dictionary.

note

Checking the spelling of a publication does not replace proofreading. If you key "form" instead of "from," the spelling checker will not detect the error.

word from the Change to list and click **Replace**. You can also key in the correct spelling of a word in the Change to box. If you want to add the new word to the dictionary, click **Add**.

- When the spelling check is complete, a message appears in the box indicating this. Click the **Close** box to close the Spelling dialog box.

Exercise 3-2

Spell check text.

1. In the Layout window, select the large text block on the page.
2. Open the Story Editor by selecting **Edit Story** on the Edit menu.
3. Check the spelling of the story by selecting **Spelling** on the Utilities menu. From the Search options, click **Current publication** and **Current story**, if necessary.
4. Click **Start**. If PageMaker indicates that "1980s" is misspelled, click **Ignore**.
5. When PageMaker indicates that "develepers" is an unknown word, click **developers** in the Change to list box, and then click **Replace**. PageMaker automatically advances to the next incorrectly spelled word. Continue the spell check and replace incorrectly spelled words.
6. When the spelling check is completed, click the **Close** box of the Spelling dialog box and return to the Layout window.
7. Save the publication as **Ex3-2** and leave it open for the next exercise.

USING THE FIND COMMAND

The Find command lets you search a publication for every occurrence of a specific character, word, or phrase. Find moves the cursor from its present position to the next occurrence of the word or phrase for which you are searching. Like the spell checking feature, you can choose to search only the selected text, one story in a publication, all stories in a publication, or all stories in all open publications.

To find a character, word, or phrase:

- In Story Editor, make sure no text is highlighted. Choose **Find** on the Utilities menu. The Find dialog box appears, as shown in Figure 3–4.
- In the Find what box, key the word or phrase you want to find.
- Click **Find**. PageMaker highlights the first occurrence.
- Click **Find next** to continue the search.
- When all occurrences have been found, the Search Completed message box appears. Click **OK**.
- Click the **Close** box to close the Find window.

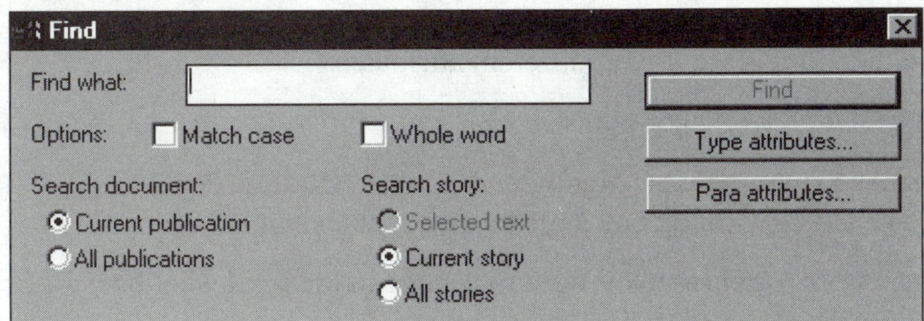

Figure 3–4
The Find dialog box is used to find a specific character, word, or phrase.

The Find command can locate whole or partial words. For example, PageMaker can find the word *all* or any word with *all* in it, such as *fall*, *horizontally*, or *alloy*. If you select the Whole word option in the Find dialog box, PageMaker limits its search to the word *all*.

Find can look for words that match a specific capitalization. For example, if you wanted to search for the word *page* in lowercase letters, you click Match case in the Find dialog box. PageMaker finds *page*, but not *Page* or *PAGE*.

The Type and Para attributes options let you find words that have specific characteristics. When you click Type Attributes, the Find Type Attributes dialog box appears, as shown in Figure 3–5. Here you can specify the font, size, width, color, or style as well as leading, tracking, and tinting of the word(s) you want to find. Type attributes are discussed in a later lesson.

When you click Para attributes, the Find Paragraph Attributes dialog box appears, as shown in Figure 3–6. You can specify the paragraph style, alignment, or leading method that you want to find. Paragraph styles are discussed in a later lesson.

Find Type Attributes
Font: Courier New
OK
Size: Any points
Leading: Any points
Cancel
Set width: Any % Size
Track: Any
Color: Any
Tint: Any %
Type style: Any Bold Underline Reverse All caps Superscript
Normal Italic Strikethru Small caps Subscript

Figure 3–5
The Find Type Attributes dialog box helps you locate words with specific type characteristics.

Find Paragraph Attributes
Paragraph style: Caption
OK
Alignment: Any
Cancel
Leading method: Any

Figure 3–6
The Find Paragraph Attributes dialog box helps you locate paragraphs with specific paragraph characteristics.

USING THE CHANGE COMMAND

The Change command is an extension of the Find command. Once you find a character, word, or phrase, you can replace it with another character, word, or phrase that you specify. The changes can be done individually or all at once.

As with the Find command, the Change command has options to search for a word with specific attributes and then to replace it with different attributes.

To find and change characters, words, or phrases:

- In Story Editor, make sure no text is highlighted. Choose **Change** on the Utilities menu. The Change dialog box appears, like that shown in Figure 3–7.
- Key the character, word, or phrase you want to change in the Find what box.
- In the Change to box, key the replacement text.
- Click **Find** to go to the first occurrence. You are asked at each occurrence if you want to change it. To continue changing the words one by one, choose **Change & find**. To replace all occurrences automatically, choose **Change all**.
- When all the occurrences have been found, click the **Close** box to close the Window, or choose another window.

Figure 3–7
The Change dialog box contains options you can use to replace a character, word, or phrase with another.

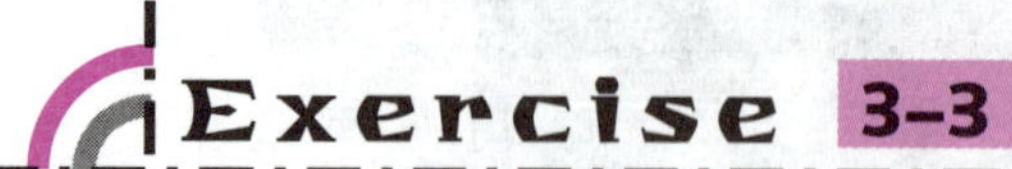

Exercise 3–3

Finding and changing text.

1. In the Layout window, select the small text block that contains the title. Open the Story Editor by selecting **Edit Story** on the Edit menu.
2. Select **Find** on the Utilities menu. Enter the word **computers** in the Find what text box. Click **Current publication** and **All stories**. Then click **Find**.
3. Click **Find next**. PageMaker also finds the word in the large text block in the publication since you selected the All stories option. Keep clicking **Find next** until a message box appears indicating the search is complete. Click **OK**.
4. In the Find dialog box, capitalize the word *computers* in the Find what box. Click the **Match case** option. Click **Find**. Click **Find next** until the search complete message box appears, and then click **OK**. Close the Find dialog box by clicking its **Close** box.
5. Select **Change** on the Utilities menu. Your last Find request is still in the Find what box. Delete it by entering **Now**. In the Change to box, key **Today,**. Click **Current publication** and **All stories**, if necessary. Click

Find. When PageMaker finds the word *Now*, click **Change & find**. When the search complete message box appears, click **OK**.

6. Click the **Close** box to close the Change dialog box.
7. Return to the Layout window.
8. Save the publication as **Ex3-3**, print it, and close it.

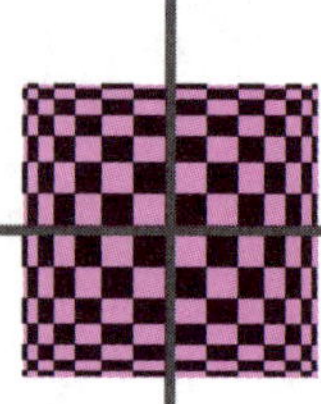

activities

❖ TRUE/FALSE

On the blank line before each sentence, place a **T** *if the statement is true and an* **F** *if it is false.*

____ 1. You can perform more editing functions in the Story Editor than you can in the Layout window.

____ 2. When you place a new story created in the Story Editor, a loaded cursor appears.

____ 3. PageMaker's spelling checker finds grammatical errors.

____ 4. PageMaker can check the spelling of only a single text block.

____ 5. With the Change & find feature, you can change only found characters, words, or phrases one at a time.

❖ COMPLETION

Answer the questions below in the space provided.

6. How do you open a new story in the Story Editor?

____

____

7. What happens to the Layout window when you select the Story Editor?

____

____

8. What does the Match case option in the Find dialog box do?

____

____

9. Which option in the Change dialog box allows you to replace all occurrences without prompts?

____

____

10. What type characteristics can you find and/or change in the Find Type Attributes dialog box?

____

____

review

Review Exercise 3-1

Use PageMaker's Story Editor.

1. Open **Exercise** from the template files. Key your heading in the top margin of the publication page.
2. Select the text block on the page and then select **Edit Story** on the Edit menu.
3. Check the spelling of the current story and make any changes necessary.
4. Find the words **worn out** and change them to **sluggish**. (*Hint:* Make sure nothing is selected in the text block; then choose **Change** on the Utilities menu.) If you are asked if you want to start the search from the beginning of the story, click **Yes**.
5. Return to Layout window.
6. If necessary, resize the text block so it fits within the page margins and move it down so it is centered on the page.
7. Save the publication as **Re3-1**.
8. Print the publication, close it, and end your PageMaker session.

Modifying Text

❖ OBJECTIVES

Upon completion of this lesson, you will be able to:

1. Choose fonts.
2. Change the size of type.
3. Change the type style of text.
4. Choose an appropriate alignment for text.
5. Apply leading.
6. Change text characteristics using the Type Specs command.

Estimated Time: 1 hour

❖ INTRODUCTION

You now know how to import text and manipulate it. In this lesson, you will learn how to change the look of your text.

❖ CHOOSING FONTS

The term *font* refers to the shape of the characters belonging to a particular family of type. A font is also called a *typeface*. A typeface with small lines added to the ends of the characters is called a *serif* typeface and is often used for main body text. A typeface without serifs is called a *sans serif* typeface and is often used for headlines (see Figure 4–1).

To change the font of text in a publication, choose Font on the Type menu and click the name of the font on the submenu. The font is applied to any new text you enter. To change the font of text that has already been keyed, you must highlight the text before choosing a new font.

You can select all the text in a text block or in a story (contained in one or more text blocks) by clicking anywhere in the text with the Text tool and then choosing the Select All command on the Edit menu.

note

There are different designs of type just as there are different designs of clothing. Text can be dressy or casual. The differences between typefaces can be obvious or subtle. You will want to choose fonts that are appropriate for your publication.

Exercise 4-1

Change the font in a publication.

1. Open **Typterm** from the template files. Maximize the window, if necessary, and key your heading in the top margin.
2. Highlight the title of the publication.

Figure 4–1
A serif typeface has small lines added to the ends of characters. Sans serif typefaces do not have the lines.

3. Change the font to **Arial** or **Helvetica** by selecting **Font** on the Type menu. If neither of these fonts is available, choose another sans serif font designated by your instructor.
4. Highlight the body of the publication. Do not highlight the title.
5. Change the font to **Times New Roman** or **Times**. If neither of these fonts is available, choose another serif font.
6. Save the publication as **Ex4-1** to the folder or disk containing your course files and leave it open for the next exercise.

❖ CHANGING TYPE SIZE

The size of type is determined by measuring its height in units called *points*. One point equals 1/72 inch.

note

A common size for body type is 12 points; however, not all 12-point type takes up the same amount of space. Point size determines the height of a letter, but design differences among type fonts may make one font wider than another.

To change the size of text you want to enter:

- Choose **Size** on the Type menu.
- Click the size on the submenu.
- Begin keying text.

To change the size of existing text:

- Highlight the text you want to change with the Text tool.
- Choose **Size** on the Type menu.
- Click the size on the submenu.

Exercise 4-2

Change the type size.

1. Highlight the title of the publication.
2. Change the size to **14** by selecting **Size** on the Type menu.
3. Highlight the body of the publication. Do not highlight the title.
4. Change the size to **12**.
5. Save the publication as **Ex4-2** and leave it open for the next exercise.

❖ CHOOSING TYPE STYLE

Type style refers to the appearance of a font. Type styles available in PageMaker are normal, boldface, italic, underline, strikethru, and reverse. Examples are shown in Figure 4–2. These styles can be applied to change the appearance of any font. For example, you might want to emphasize a specific word by applying a boldface style to it. More than one style can be applied to the same text. For example, you can boldface and italicize text.

This is an example of normal text.

This is an example of bold text.

This is an example of italic text.

<u>This is an example of underlined text.</u>

~~This is an example of strikethru text.~~

Figure 4–2
Type styles are used to emphasize text.

To change the style of text you want to enter:

- Choose **Type Style** on the Type menu.
- Click the type style on the submenu.
- Begin keying text.

To change the style of existing text:

- Highlight the text you want to change with the Text tool.
- Choose **Type Style** on the Type menu.
- Click the type style on the submenu.

You might find it easier to use keyboard shortcuts to change the style of text. Table 4–1 lists the shortcuts.

Style	Windows Shortcut	Macintosh Shortcut
Normal	Shift + Ctrl + Spacebar	Shift + Command + Spacebar
Bold	Shift + Ctrl + B	Shift + Command + B
Italic	Shift + Ctrl + I	Shift + Command + I
Underline	Shift + Ctrl + U	Shift + Command + U
Strikethru	Shift + Ctrl + S	Shift + Command + /
Reverse	Shift + Ctrl + V	Shift + Command + V

Table 4–1
Keyboard shortcuts

Exercise 4-3

Change the style of text.

1. Highlight the title of the publication.
2. Boldface the title by selecting **Type Style** on the Type menu and then **Bold**.
3. Boldface the subheading *Characters* and all other subheadings in the publication. Do not boldface the periods following each subheading.
4. Italicize the word **character** in the first sentence of the first paragraph.
5. Italicize the word **baseline** in the first sentence of the second paragraph.
6. Italicize the word **descender** in the first sentence of the third paragraph. Also italicize the characters **g** and **y** in the next sentence.
7. Italicize the word **x-height** in the second sentence of the fourth paragraph.
8. Italicize the word **ascender** in the first sentence of the fifth paragraph and the characters **f** and **k** in the next sentence.
9. Italicize the words **cap height** in the first sentence of the sixth paragraph.
10. Italicize the word **serifs** in the second sentence of the seventh paragraph. Also italicize the word **sans serif** in the fourth sentence of the seventh paragraph.
11. Save the publication as **Ex4-3** and leave it open for the next exercise.

❖ SETTING ALIGNMENT

You can align text so that it is centered in the text block, aligned with the left margin or right margin, or justified so that is flush with both margins. In addition, you have the choice of force justification. Force justification is used when a short line—perhaps at the end of a paragraph—needs to be spread across empty space. Figure 4–3 illustrates the different alignments. The default alignment is left alignment.

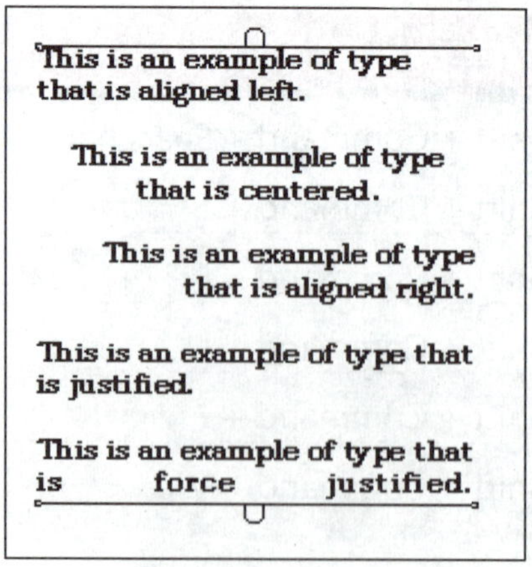

This is an example of type
that is aligned left.

This is an example of type
that is centered.

This is an example of type
that is aligned right.

This is an example of type that
is justified.

This is an example of type that
is force justified.

Figure 4–3
Alignment determines the placement on a line of text.

To set the alignment for text you want to enter:

- Choose **Alignment** on the Type menu.
- Click the alignment option on the submenu.
- Begin keying the new text.

To change the alignment of existing text:

- Highlight the text you want to align with the Text tool.
- Choose **Alignment** on the Type menu.
- Click the alignment option on the submenu.

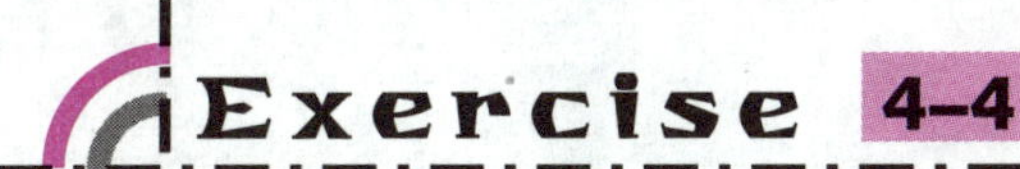

Change the alignment of text.

1. Highlight the title of the publication.
2. Change the alignment to **Align Center** by selecting **Alignment** on the Type menu.
3. Highlight the body of the publication.
4. Change the alignment to **Justify**.
5. Save the publication as **Ex4-4** and leave it open for the next exercise.

CHANGING LEADING

Spacing is an important part of page layout. Adding or deleting space in text can visually enhance your publication. The amount of space between lines of type is called *leading*. To change leading, you use the Leading command on the Type menu, as shown in Figure 4–4. The default leading is Auto, which sets the leading at a number 20 percent larger than the size of the font you are using. It is equivalent to single-spaced text. To double space your text, set the leading at about twice the type size.

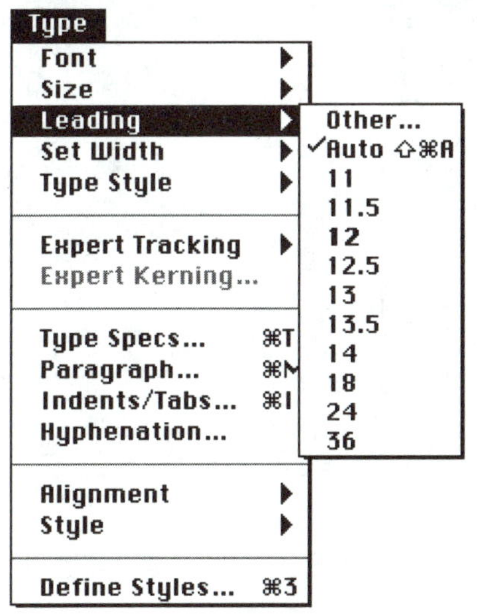

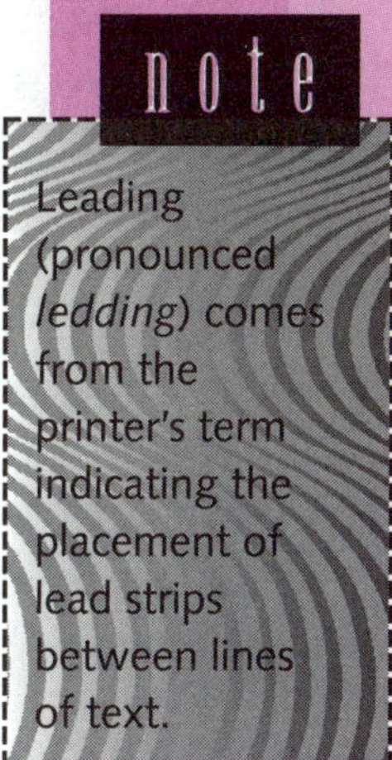

Figure 4–4
The Leading command allows you to change the spacing between lines of text, which can make the text easier to read.

To set the leading for text you want to enter:

- Choose **Leading** on the Type menu.
- Select the leading on the submenu.
- Key the new text.

To change the leading of existing text:

- Highlight the text you want to change with the Text tool.
- Choose **Leading** on the Type menu.
- Select the leading on the submenu.

Change the leading of text.

1. Highlight all the text by choosing **Select All** on the Edit menu.
2. Change the leading to **21** by selecting **Leading** on the Type menu.
3. Save the publication as **Ex4-5** and leave it open for the next exercise.

❖ CHANGING TYPE SPECS

When you want to change several text attributes at the same time, you can use the Type Specs command on the Type menu. The Type Specifications dialog box appears like that shown in Figure 4–5. In the Type Specifications dialog box, you can change the font, size, leading, color (if you have a color monitor or printer), and style of text. You can change the leading or size to a point that is not listed by keying the point in the leading or size box. You can key in a value in increments of one-tenth of a point, such as 12.5.

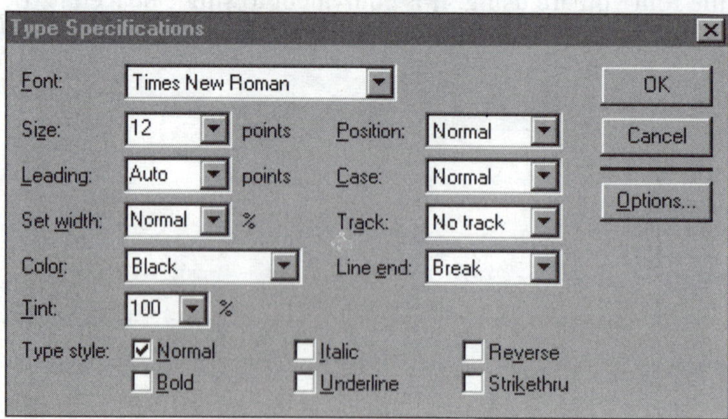

Figure 4–5 The Type Specifications dialog box allows you to change the font, size, type style, and other characteristics of text at the same time.

Exercise 4–6

Change the type specs of text.

1. Highlight the body of the publication. Do not highlight the title.
2. Select **Type Specs** on the Type menu.
3. Change the type size to **11** and change the leading to **22**. Click **OK**.
4. Save the publication as **Ex4-6**.
5. Print the publication and then close it.

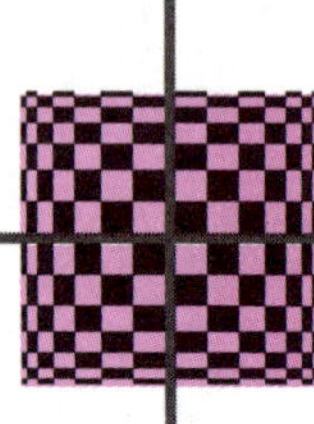

activities

❖ TRUE/FALSE

On the blank line before each sentence, place a **T** *if the statement is true and an* **F** *if it is false.*

____ 1. A font is also called a typeface.

____ 2. The size of type is determined by measuring its height in units called points.

____ 3. You can emphasize a word by applying a boldface style to it.

____ 4. Choosing justified text centers text between the right and left margins.

____ 5. Leading can be used to add space between lines of text.

❖ COMPLETION

Answer the questions below in the space provided.

6. What determines the fonts you select for a publication?

____

____

7. If no text is highlighted when a font is chosen, what is affected by the new font choice?

____

____

8. When would you use special type styles?

____

____

9. What is the purpose of adding more leading to a paragraph?

____

____

10. What does the Type Specifications dialog box allow you to do?

____

____

review

Review Exercise 4-1

Apply attributes to text.

1. Open **Bday** from the template files. Enter your heading in the top margin. If the heading defaults to centered alignment, highlight it and change it to **Align Left**.
2. Highlight the text block and change the alignment to **Align Center**.
3. Change the view if necessary, and boldface **Hannah Richards**.
4. Italicize the last line, which begins *Please limit*.
5. Using the Type Specifications dialog box, change the font of the entire text block to **Arial**, **Helvetica**, or a similar serif font, and the size to **30** points.
6. Adjust the placement of the text block, if necessary.
7. Save the publication as **Re4-1** to the folder or disk containing your course files.
8. Print the publication, close it, and end your PageMaker session.

Applying Advanced Text Modification Techniques

❖ OBJECTIVES

Upon completion of this lesson, you will be able to:

1. Modify text using the Control Palette.
2. Use tracking.
3. Kern text manually and automatically.
4. Change the width of characters.

Estimated Time: 1 hour

❖ INTRODUCTION

In the previous lesson, you learned how to modify the basic look of text using commands on the Type menu and keyboard shortcuts. In this lesson, you will learn other ways to change the appearance of text. In addition, you will learn to use the Control Palette to quickly and easily make multiple changes to the text.

❖ USING THE CONTROL PALETTE FOR TEXT

PageMaker's Control Palette is a handy tool you use to apply a variety of formatting characteristics to text and objects. The functions you can perform using Control Palette buttons vary, depending on the tool currently selected in the toolbox.

To display the Control Palette, select it on the Window menu. If the Text tool is currently selected, the Control Palette looks like that shown in Figure 5–1. Many of the buttons might look familiar to you since you have already practiced applying text attributes, such as type sizes and styles, in the previous lesson. The Apply button on the Control Palette changes to indicate the tool selection. When the Text tool is selected, an icon of the I-beam appears.

Notice the "A" button and paragraph marker (¶) button to the right of the Apply button. Clicking the A button activates type specifications on the Control Palette, as shown in Figure 5–1. Clicking the paragraph button activates paragraph specifications, such as alignment, indents, and spacing between paragraphs. You'll use these in the next lesson.

Figure 5–1
The Control Palette can be used to change most type or paragraph specifications.

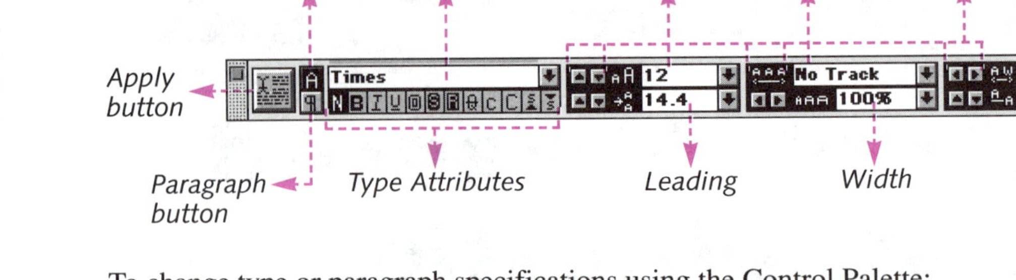

> **note**
>
> You can move the Control Palette to another location on the screen by clicking on the vertical bar below the Close box on the left side of the palette and then dragging.

To change type or paragraph specifications using the Control Palette:

- Choose the **Control Palette** on the Window menu.
- Select the **Text** tool and highlight the text to be changed.
- Select the **A** or **¶** button.
- Select the specification you want to change. Click the arrow on the right side of the option box to display a list of choices, or enter a new specification in the text box. You can also use the nudge buttons, represented by the arrows to the left of the option, to change values in small increments.
- In some cases, you see changes applied to text as you make them. You can also click the **Apply** button or press **Enter** (Windows) or **Return** (Macintosh) to apply modifications.
- To Close the Control Palette, click its **Close** box, or choose **Control Palette** on the Window menu.

Exercise 5–1

Use the Control Palette to change text.

1. Open **Cities** from the template files.
2. Display the **Control Palette** by selecting it on the Window menu.
3. Select the Text tool from the toolbox. Notice how the buttons available in the Control Palette change.
4. Highlight *New York*.
5. Delete the value in the type size box by highlighting it and keying **150**. Click **Apply**.
6. Nudge the size down to **149.4** by clicking on the down-pointing nudge button to the left of the type size box.
7. In the font box, click the arrow to display the font selection. Choose a sans serif typeface, such as **Helvetica** or **Arial**.
8. Save the publication as **Ex5-1** to the folder or disk containing your course files and leave it open for the next exercise.

❖ SELECTING TRACKING

You can enhance the appearance of text by modifying the space between characters. This is referred to as *tracking*. Tracking can be useful when you need to fit type into limited space.

You can use the Tracking option on the Control Palette to change tracking (see Figure 5–1). You can also use the Expert Tracking command on the Type menu (see Figure 5–2).You can change the spacing between characters from Very Loose to Very Tight, as illustrated in Figure 5–3. The default tracking is No Track, which uses the built-in spacing of the font you are using.

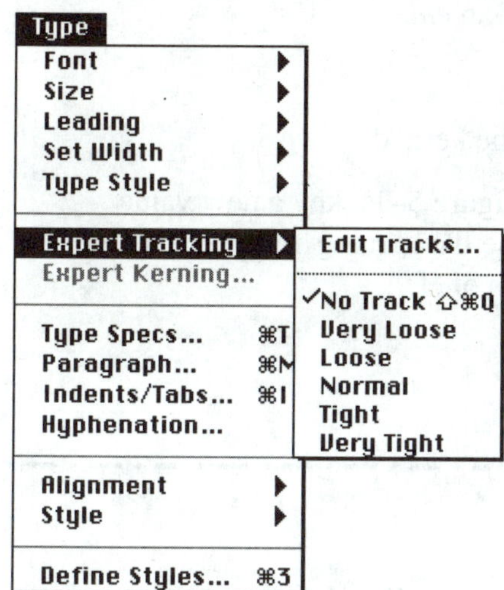

Figure 5–2
Tracking options on the Type menu

Tracking - No Track
Tracking - Very Loose
Tracking - Loose
Tracking - Normal
Tracking - Tight
Tracking - Very Tight

Figure 5–3
Samples of tracking applied to type

To apply tracking:

- Highlight the text you want to track with the **Text** tool.
- Click the **Tracking** button on the Control Palette or choose **Expert Tracking** on the Type menu.
- Select the desired tracking option.

Exercise 5–2

Change tracking.

1. Highlight **New York** with the **Text** tool.
2. On the Control Palette, click the **Tracking** button and then click **Normal**.
3. Save the publication as **Ex5-2** and leave it open for the next exercise.

❖ ADJUSTING KERNING

Tracking assigns an equal amount of space between each character in the selected text. With *kerning*, you can change spacing between a pair of characters.

Letters that are frequently kerned—called *kerning pairs*— include LA, Po, To, Tr, Ta, Tu, Te, Ty, Wa, WA, We, we, Wo, Ya, Yo, and yo. Reducing the space between these letters enhances the text's appearance, especially for large-size type like that used in headlines and titles. PageMaker lets you kern manually and automatically.

Kerning spacing is measured in *ems*. An *em* is a printer's term for a horizontal space approximately ⅙ of an inch. An *en* is half the width of an *em*.

To increase or decrease spacing between letters:

- Click the I-beam between the two characters to be kerned.
- In the Kerning box on the Control Palette (see Figure 5–1), key a new value between –1 em and +1 em to decrease or increase the kerning value, or use the nudge buttons to change the values in increments of .1.

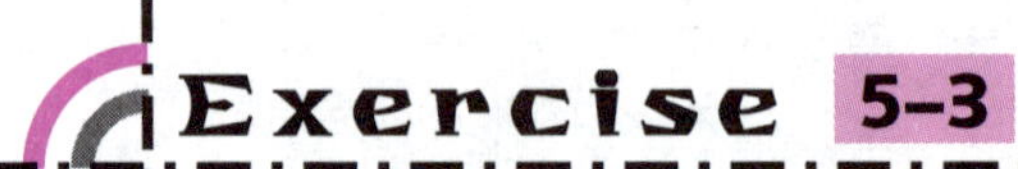

Exercise 5-3

Adjust kerning.

1. Select the **Text** tool and click the I-beam between the **Y** and the **o** in *New York*.
2. In the Kerning box on the Control Palette, highlight **0** and key **-.15** to reduce the space between these two letters. Press **Enter** (Windows) or **Return** (Macintosh).
3. Use the Kerning nudge button on the Control Palette to add **.03** ems of space between the r and the k in *York*.
4. Save the publication as **Ex5-3** and leave it open for the next exercise.

AUTOMATIC KERNING

When a typeface is designed, the creator determines the appropriate spacing between kerning pairs. Automatic kerning in PageMaker lets you apply this spacing to kerning pairs in selected text. Because kerning is usually only apparent at larger point sizes, PageMaker lets you determine a point size above which automatic kerning is applied.

To apply automatic kerning:

- Select the paragraph to be kerned automatically.
- Select **Paragraph** on the Type menu. The Paragraph Specifications dialog box appears, like that shown in Figure 5–4. Click the **Spacing** button.
- The Paragraph Spacing Attributes dialog box appears, like that shown in Figure 5–5. Click the **Auto Above** box and specify the point size above which you want PageMaker to kern pairs.
- Click **OK** twice to return to your publication.

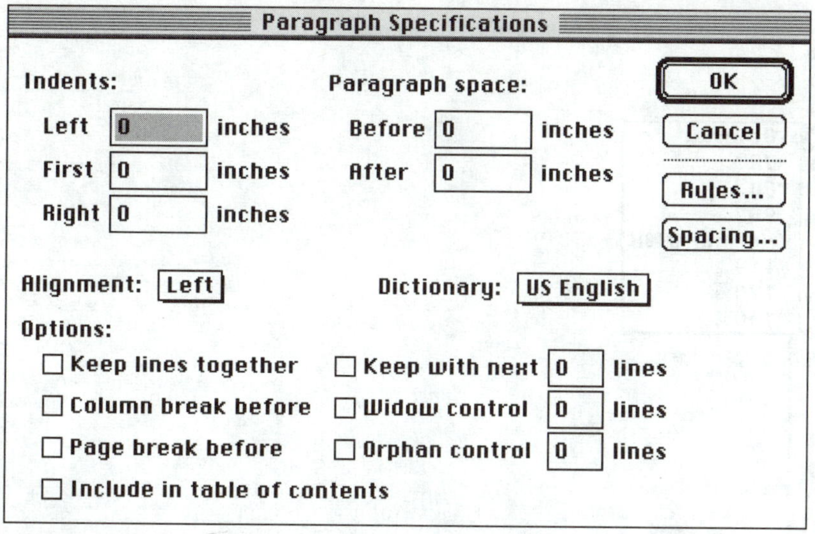

Paragraph Specifications

Indents: Left 0 inches; First 0 inches; Right 0 inches
Paragraph space: Before 0 inches; After 0 inches
OK | Cancel | Rules... | Spacing...
Alignment: Left
Dictionary: US English
Options:
☐ Keep lines together ☐ Keep with next 0 lines
☐ Column break before ☐ Widow control 0 lines
☐ Page break before ☐ Orphan control 0 lines
☐ Include in table of contents

Figure 5–4 Paragraph Specifications dialog box

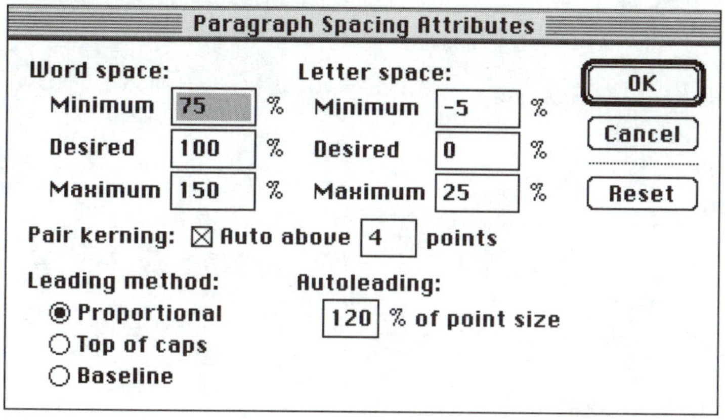

Paragraph Spacing Attributes

Word space: Minimum 75 %; Desired 100 %; Maximum 150 %
Letter space: Minimum -5 %; Desired 0 %; Maximum 25 %
OK | Cancel | Reset
Pair kerning: ☒ Auto above 4 points
Leading method: ◉ Proportional ○ Top of caps ○ Baseline
Autoleading: 120 % of point size

Figure 5–5 Apply automatic kerning in the Paragraph Spacing Attributes dialog box.

Exercise 5–4

Apply automatic kerning.

1. Highlight the word **Texas**. Notice the extra space between the T and e.
2. Select **Paragraph** on the Type menu and click **Spacing**.
3. Click the **Auto Above** box and then enter **12** in the points box.
4. Click **OK** twice to return to the publication page. The space between the T and the e is automatically kerned.
5. Save the publication as **Ex5-4** and leave it open for the next exercise.

❖ SETTING CHARACTER WIDTH

The Width option on the Control Palette lets you change the width of characters. You can also use the Set Width command on the Type menu, as shown in Figure 5–6.

As shown in Figure 5–7, you can set widths at 70 percent to 130 percent of the typeface's normal width. You can specify a character width other than those listed by choosing Other and keying the new percentage.

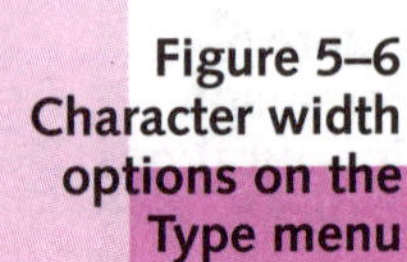

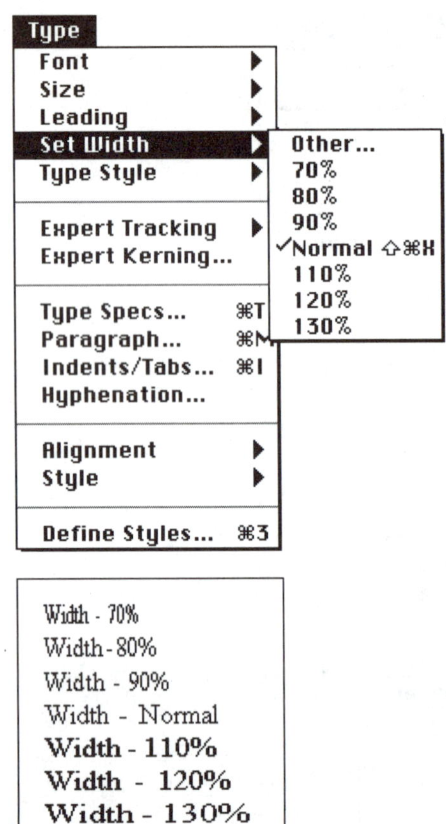

Figure 5–6
Character width options on the Type menu

Width - 70%
Width - 80%
Width - 90%
Width - Normal
Width - 110%
Width - 120%
Width - 130%

Figure 5–7
Examples of widths applied to type

To set the width of characters:

- Highlight the text with the **Text** tool.
- Click the **Width** button on the Control Palette or choose **Set Width** on the Type menu.
- Click the desired width.

Exercise 5–5

Change the width of text.

1. Highlight the word **Texas.**
2. Choose **Set Width** on the Type menu. Select **120%**.
3. Set the width of the words *New York* to **80%** by clicking the **Width** button on the Control Palette.
4. Save the publication as **Ex5-5**.
5. Print the publication and then close it.

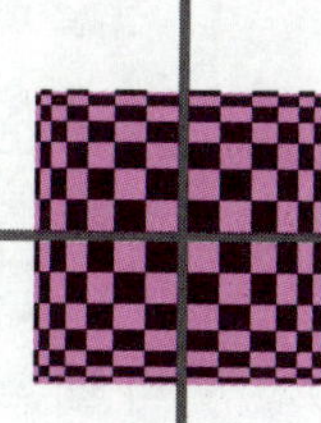

activities

❖ TRUE/FALSE

On the blank line before each sentence, place a **T** *if the statement is true and an* **F** *if it is false.*

____ 1. The Control Palette is opened by selecting it on the Type menu.

____ 2. Tracking is used to change the amount of space between paragraphs.

____ 3. Kerning changes the amount of space between lines of text.

____ 4. Setting the width of a character changes the amount of space the actual letter uses.

____ 5. The Control Palette options vary, depending on the tool currently selected from the toolbox.

❖ COMPLETION

Answer the questions below in the space provided.

6. How do you move the Control Palette to another location on the screen?

____

____

7. What button on the Control Palette must you select to activate the text characteristics options?

____

____

8. What is the difference between tracking and kerning?

____

____

9. What is an "em"?

____

____

10. What is one method for changing the width of a character?

____

____

review

Review Exercise 5-1

Use advanced text modification techniques.

1. Open **Question** from the template files.
2. Display the Control Palette and change the size of the text in the top text block to **72**. Change the tracking to **Very Loose**. Boldface the text.
3. Move the bottom text block so that the bottom border rests on the bottom margin.
4. Change the size of the text in the bottom text block to **24**. Change the leading to **36**. Move the text block again so that the bottom border rests on the bottom margin.
5. Change the size of the top question mark to **100** points.
6. Change the size of the middle question mark to **200** points and set its width to **130%**.
7. Change the size of the bottom question mark to **150** points and change its width to **110%**.
8. Use kerning to change the space between the Y and O in YOU to **-.2**, and the space between the O and the U to **-.1**.
9. Save the publication as **Re5-1**.
10. Print the publication, close it, and end your PageMaker session.

Formatting Paragraphs

❖ OBJECTIVES

Upon completion of this lesson, you will be able to:

1. Set automatic and hanging indents.
2. Set tabs.
3. Determine appropriate hyphenation.
4. Use paragraph specifications.
5. Use the Control Palette to format paragraphs.

Estimated Time: 1 hour

❖ INTRODUCTION

Changing the look of paragraphs adds interest to your publication. In this lesson, you will learn how to apply more advanced formatting techniques to paragraphs of text.

❖ SETTING INDENTS

Indents are commonly used to indicate the beginning of a new paragraph, but you can indent any selected text any amount of space you want.

You set an indent by selecting Indents/Tabs on the Type menu. The Indents/Tabs dialog box appears, as shown in Figure 6–1. Indents are applied only to the paragraph in which the cursor is located unless additional paragraphs have been highlighted. The triangles that appear on the ruler reflect the indents and tabs that have been applied to selected text.

On the far left side of the ruler are two black triangles called *indent icons*. The top triangle controls the indent of the first line of a paragraph, and the bottom triangle controls the indent of the left margin of the remainder of the paragraph. A single triangle on the right controls the right margin of the paragraph.

Dragging the first-line indent icon toward the right allows you to indent automatically the first line of the selected paragraph. To create a hanging indent—that is, all of the paragraph *except* for the first line is indented—you drag the left margin indent icon to the right.

You will notice that when you try to drag the left margin indent icon, the first-line indent icon moves also. To avoid this, position the left margin indent icon first, and then move the first-line icon to the desired location. You can also hold down the shift key while dragging the left margin indent icon to prevent the first-line icon from moving.

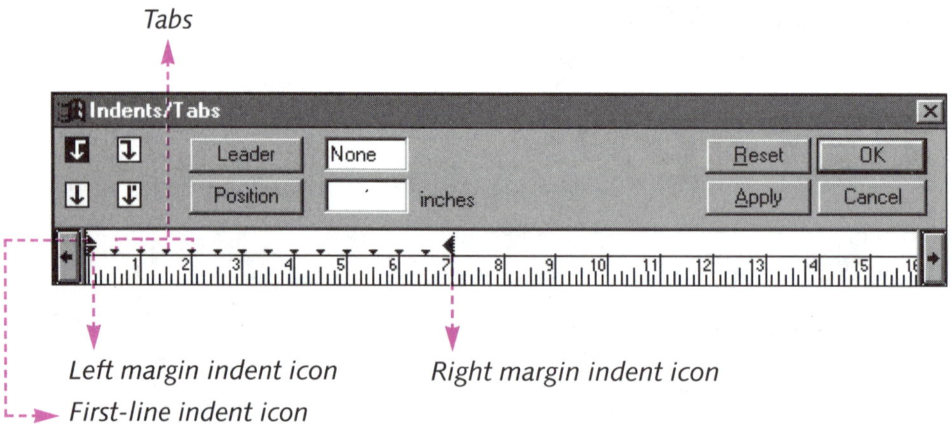

Tabs

Indents/Tabs
Leader None Reset OK
Position inches Apply Cancel

Left margin indent icon
Right margin indent icon
First-line indent icon

Figure 6–1
The Indents/Tabs option allows you to change indents.

Exercise 6-1

Add a first-line indent to a paragraph.

1. Open **Palette** from the template files.
2. Highlight the first paragraph with the **Text** tool.
3. Choose **Indents/Tabs** on the Type menu.
4. Drag the first-line indent icon to the **.25**-inch mark on the ruler. The Position indicator shows where the icon is positioned on the ruler. Click **OK**.
5. Save the publication as **Ex6-1** to the folder or disk containing your course files and leave it open for the next exercise.

❖ SETTING TABS

Tabs can be added, deleted, and moved using the options in the Indents/Tabs dialog box. As shown in Figure 6–2, there are four types of tabs: left tabs, right tabs, center tabs, and decimal tabs. With a left tab, text is aligned left at the tab stop. With a right tab, text is aligned right at the tab stop. With a center tab, text is aligned center at the tab stop. With a decimal tab, numbers are aligned at their decimal points at the tab stop.

PageMaker has preset tabs every ½ inch. Notice in Figure 6–2 that the preset tabs are designated by small triangles. If you click one of the preset tabs, all tabs to the left of the selected tab are removed and an arrow appears, indicating the type of the new tab. Those to the right remain unchanged. You choose the type of tab from the tab icons in the dialog box. At least one tab must show on the ruler at all times.

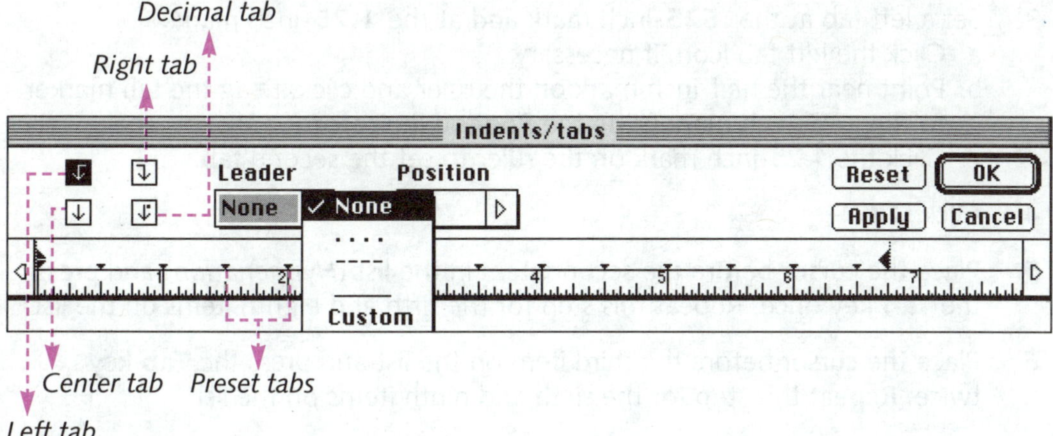

Figure 6–2
Tab icons and default tab stops

To change a tab:

- Select **Indents/Tabs** on the Type menu.
- To add a tab, click the type of tab you want and then click a position on the Indents/Tabs ruler.
- To remove a tab, click the tab and drag it off the Indents/Tabs ruler. It disappears.
- To move a tab, click the tab and drag it to the new location. The Position indicator shows you to what point on the ruler the tab is being moved.
- To reset the Indents/Tabs ruler to the preset tabs, click **Reset**.
- Click **OK** to return to the screen.
- Press the **Tab** key to apply the tabs you've set.

You can add *leaders* between tabs to enhance the readability of tabbed text. A frequently used leader is a dotted line that helps draw the eye across the page to a tabbed item.

To place a leader before a tab:

- On the ruler, click the tab to be preceded by the leader.
- Click the **Leader** option in the Indents/Tabs dialog box. See Figure 6–2. A list of different leaders appears.
- Select the leader style you want.
- Click **OK**.

note

The Indents/Tabs ruler changes, depending upon the view you have chosen. If you are using Actual size, the ruler will be 5 inches wide and must be scrolled in order to see the tabs across the entire page. If you are using Fit in Window view, you can see all the tabs.

Exercise 6–2

Set tabs for a paragraph.

1. Highlight the bulleted text below the opening paragraph.
2. Choose **Indents/Tabs** on the Type menu.

3. Set a left tab at the **.625**-inch mark and at the **1.25**-inch mark:
   a. Click the left tab icon, if necessary.
   b. Point near the half-inch mark on the ruler and click. Drag the tab marker to the .625-inch mark using the Position indicator.
   c. Click the 1.25-inch mark on the ruler to set the second tab.
4. Click **OK**.
5. Place the cursor before the second item in the list (*Hyphenation*) and press the **Tab** key once. Repeat this step for the fifth and eighth items on the list.
6. Place the cursor before the third item on the list and press the **Tab** key twice. Repeat this step for the sixth and ninth items on the list.
7. Highlight the bulleted text again.
8. Choose **Indents/Tabs** on the Type menu.
9. Change the tab at the 1.25-inch mark to a tab with a leader:
   a. Click the tab marker.
   b. Click **Leader** and selected the dotted line leader.
   c. Click **Apply** to see the changes. Click **Cancel**.
10. Save the publication as **Ex6-2** and leave it open for the next exercise.

❖ CHOOSING HYPHENATION OPTIONS

Because of PageMaker's automatic wordwrap feature, long words that are bumped to the next line of text can leave a distracting gap in the line above. To remedy this, PageMaker has an automatic hyphenation option that is turned on by default.

If you want to turn off the hyphenation option (for example, in headlines where hyphens are not appropriate) or to change hyphenation procedures, select Hyphenation on the Type menu. The Hyphenation dialog box appears, as shown in Figure 6–3. To turn off hyphenation, click Off and then click OK. To turn on hyphenation, click On and then click OK.

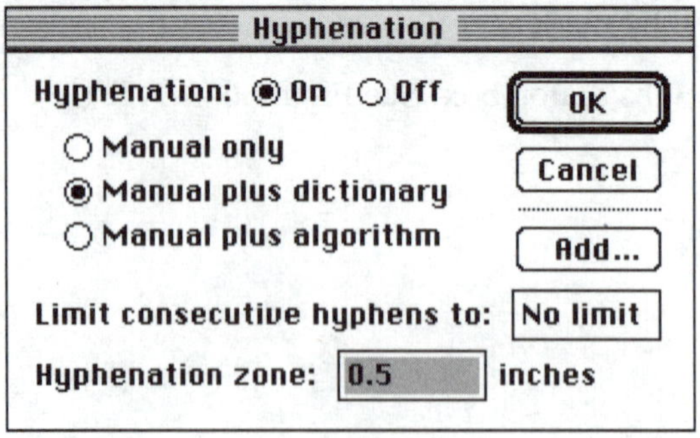

Hyphenation
Hyphenation: ◉ On ○ Off
○ Manual only
◉ Manual plus dictionary
○ Manual plus algorithm
OK
Cancel
Add...
Limit consecutive hyphens to: No limit
Hyphenation zone: 0.5 inches

Figure 6–3 You can turn on and off PageMaker's hypenation feature.

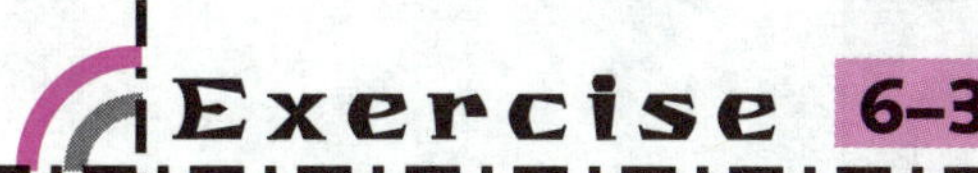

Turn off hyphenation.

1. Highlight all the text in the publication. Notice the hyphenation used in the top paragraph.
2. Select **Hyphenation** on the Type menu and click **Off**. Then click **OK**.
3. Save the publication as **Ex6-3** and leave it open for the next exercise.

❖ USING PARAGRAPH SPECIFICATIONS

Just as you used options in the Type Specifications dialog box to apply various attributes to text at the same time, you can use options in the Paragraph Specifications dialog box to apply formatting to a paragraph. The Paragraph Specifications dialog box is shown in Figure 6–4. To open it, select Paragraph on the Type menu.

Paragraph Specifications

Indents: Left 0 inches; First 0 inches; Right 0 inches

Paragraph space: Before 0 inches; After 0 inches

OK | Cancel | Rules... | Spacing...

Alignment: Left   Dictionary: US English

Options:
- ☐ Keep lines together
- ☐ Column break before
- ☐ Page break before
- ☐ Include in table of contents
- ☐ Keep with next 0 lines
- ☐ Widow control 0 lines
- ☐ Orphan control 0 lines

Figure 6–4
You can apply various formats to paragraphs in the Paragraph Specifications dialog box.

You can set the left and right margins and indent the first line by entering the number of inches for each in the Indents boxes. In addition, you can select alignment.

The amount of space between paragraphs can be set using the Before and After Paragraph space options. Clicking the Rules option displays the Paragraph Rules dialog box (see Figure 6–5) where you can select a rule line to place above or below a paragraph and choose the line style.

Other options in the Paragraph Specifications dialog box let you choose how many lines to keep together when flowing text from one column to another or from one page to another and when to break text on a page or in a column. Selecting Widow control and Orphan control removes widows (the last line of a text block bumped to the top of a page or column) and orphans (the first line of a text block left stranded at the bottom of a page or column) from your document.

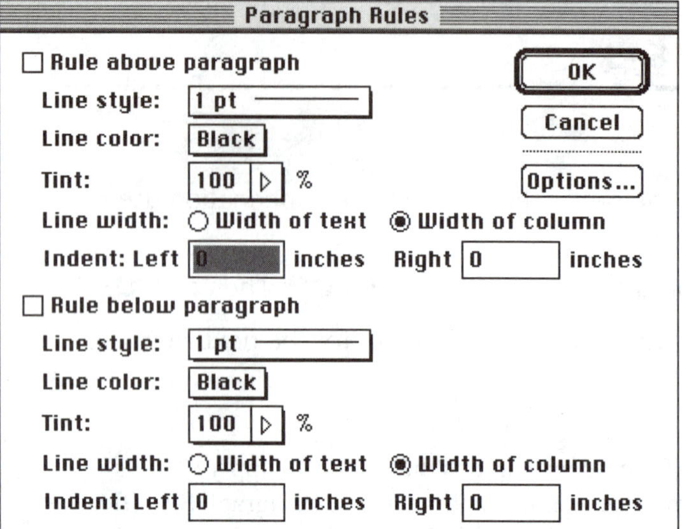

Figure 6–5 The Paragraph Rules dialog box lets you add lines above and below

Use options in the Paragraph Specifications dialog box.

1. Highlight the first paragraph.
2. Select **Paragraph** on the Type menu.
3. In the Paragraph Specifications dialog box, click **Rules**.
4. In the Paragraph Rules dialog box, click the **Rule below paragraph** option.
5. For the Line style, scroll to the **6pt triple line** and select it.
6. Click **Options**.
7. In the Bottom box, highlight **Auto** and key **.5**. Click OK three times to return to the publication page.
8. Save the publication as **Ex6-4** and leave it open for the next activity.

❖ USING THE CONTROL PALETTE TO FORMAT PARAGRAPHS

Another way to change the attributes of a paragraph is with the Control Palette. Just as you used this palette to modify text attributes, you can use it to modify paragraphs. When you select the paragraph button (¶) on the Control Palette, the palette appears like that shown in Figure 6–6.

You can change paragraph styles, indentations, spaces before and after the paragraph, and alignment.

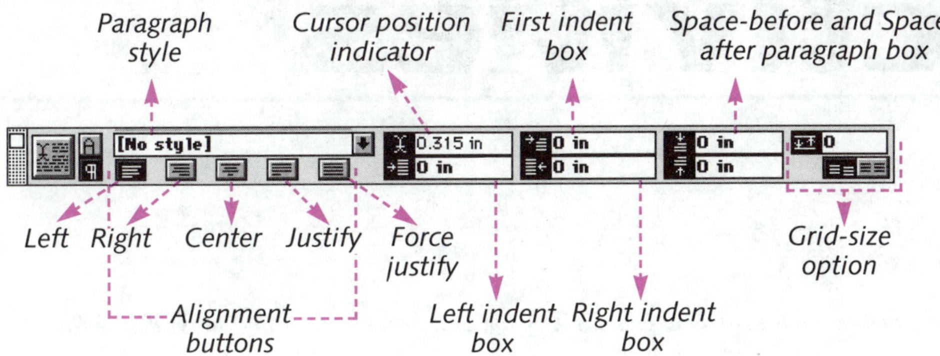

Figure 6–6
The Control Palette can be used to change paragraph attributes.

Exercise 6–5

Use the Control Palette to set paragraph specifications.

1. Open the **Control Palette** by selecting it on the Window menu. Click the ¶ button.
2. Select the text in the bulleted list.
3. In the Space-after paragraph box, highlight **0**, and enter **.1** inch. Click **Apply**.
4. Select the first paragraph. Change its alignment to **Justify**. (Make sure you don't accidentally select the Force justify button.)
5. Close the **Control Palette**.
6. Save the publication as **Ex6-5**.
7. Print the publication and then close it.

activities

❖ TRUE/FALSE

On the blank line before each sentence, place a **T** *if the statement is true and an* **F** *if it is false.*

____ 1. The Indents/Tabs command is on the Type menu.

____ 2. The first-line indent icon and the left margin indent icon on the Indents/Tabs ruler are used to set tabs.

____ 3. PageMaker automatically presets tabs at 1-inch intervals.

____ 4. Hyphenation is important as a means of reducing the gaps in spacing at the end of a line.

____ 5. The Paragraph Specifications dialog box and the Control Palette provide paragraph formatting options.

❖ COMPLETION

Answer the questions below in the space provided.

6. What is the purpose of leaders?

____

____

7. What are the four types of tabs? Define them.

____

____

8. When would you want to turn off hyphenation?

____

____

9. What is the Rules option in the Paragraph Specifications dialog box?

____

____

10. What attributes does the Control Palette for paragraphs allow you to modify?

____

____

review

Review Exercise 6-1

Change paragraph attributes.

1. Open **Banquet** from the template files.
2. Highlight all the text.
3. Choose **Indents/Tabs** on the Type menu. Set a left tab at .5 inches and a left tab with leader dots at 1 inch and at 2.5 inches. Click **OK**.
4. Press **Tab** once for each of the items under the dinner menu.
5. Press **Tab** again for the *Coffee* and *Tea* items.
6. Highlight the title. Turn off the hyphenation.
7. Open the Paragraph Specifications dialog box and center the top two lines.
8. Open the **Control Palette**.
9. Align to the right the line that begins *Introduction*. Do the same to the lines beginning with *Dinner Music*, *Guest Speaker*, and *Closing Remarks*.
10. Center the word *Dinner* and change the space after it to **.2** inches.
11. Center the bottom line.
12. Close the **Control Palette**.
13. Save the publication as **Re6-1** to the folder or disk containing your course files.
14. Print the publication, close it, and end your PageMaker session.

lesson 7

Adding Graphics to a Publication

❖ OBJECTIVES

Upon completion of this lesson, you will be able to:

1. Cut, copy, and paste graphic objects.
2. Import graphic objects.
3. Draw simple graphics.
4. Change the line and fill of a graphic.
5. Round corners.
6. Layer objects.
7. Group and ungroup objects.
8. Lock objects in place.

Estimated Time: 1 hour

❖ INTRODUCTION

PageMaker treats individual elements on the screen as objects. This includes text blocks as well as graphics. You have already learned to work with text blocks. In this lesson, you will learn to work with graphic objects. Combining text and graphics to create different types of publications is the basis of desktop publishing.

❖ CUTTING, COPYING, AND PASTING GRAPHICS

Before you actually create your own graphics using the drawing tools in the toolbox, let's review some basics on how to place and manipulate objects on a page.

You can cut, copy, and paste graphics using the same methods you did with text. Cutting an object removes it from its current location and places it on the Clipboard until you paste it to a new location. Copying an object leaves the original in place but lets you paste a duplicate in another location. To move or copy a graphic to another page or document, you can use the cut, copy, and paste commands. To move an object on a page, you simply select the object and drag it to the new location.

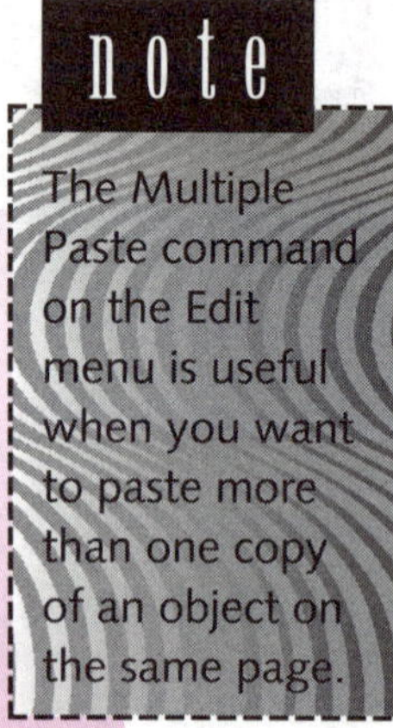

note

The Multiple Paste command on the Edit menu is useful when you want to paste more than one copy of an object on the same page.

To cut or copy an object and then place it in a new location:

- Click the Pointer tool and select the object you want to move.
- Choose **Cut** or **Copy** on the Edit menu.
- Move the pointer to the new location and click.
- Choose **Paste** on the Edit menu.
- Reposition the object by dragging it to the position desired, if necessary.

INLINE AND INDEPENDENT GRAPHICS

An *independent graphic* is one that can be moved about the page independently of a text block. An *inline graphic* is one that is embedded in a text block. Once embedded, it becomes a part of a text block and moves with the text.

To create an inline graphic:

- Copy an independent graphic.
- Select the **Text** tool and click the I-beam in the text where you want the graphic to appear.
- Select **Paste** on the Edit menu.

Exercise 7-1

Paste a graphic in a publication.

1. Open **Icecream** from the template files.
2. With the **Pointer** tool, select the ice cream cone on the pasteboard.
3. Select **Cut** on the Edit menu.
4. Choose the **Text** tool and click the I-beam after the word *galore*. Press the **Spacebar**.
5. Select **Paste** on the Edit menu. The ice cream cone is now an inline graphic.
6. Save the publication as **Ex7-1** to the folder or disk containing your course files and leave it open for the next exercise.

note

PageMaker imports a variety of graphic formats: BMP, PCX, CGM, WMF, PNT, PICT, TIFF, and EPS. You may see these letters used as extensions on filenames of imported graphics.

❖ IMPORTING OBJECTS

In Lesson 2, you learned how to import text using the Place command on the File menu. Just as you can import text, you can import graphics that have been created in a variety of other programs supported by PageMaker. Once you have imported these graphics, they can be modified somewhat using PageMaker tools.

To import an object:

- Choose **Place** on the File menu. It is important to note that if the Pointer tool is selected, you can place only an independent graphic. If the Text tool is selected, you can place the graphic as an independent graphic or as an inline graphic.

- Choose the file you want to place.
- If necessary, select from the Place options the way you want the graphic to be placed—as inline or independent.
- Click **Open** (Windows) or **OK** (Macintosh).
- If you selected the independent graphic option, a loaded graphic icon like the one shown appears. Click where you want the object to be placed. (Note that the icon may differ, depending on the tool used to create the object.)

note

PageMaker can establish a link to the original document in which a graphic or text was created. If a link is established, you can modify the original after you import it into PageMaker, and the changes are reflected in PageMaker. For more information, open the PageMaker Help facility and conduct a search for *Linking*.

Exercise 7-2

Import a graphic to a publication.

1. Choose the **Text** tool and click after the word *fruit*.
2. Choose **Place** on the File menu.
3. Select **Strberry** from the template files. Make sure the **As inline graphic** option is selected. Click **Open** or **OK**. A strawberry is placed in the text.
4. Select the **Pointer** tool and choose **Place** on the File menu.
5. Select **Sundae** from the template files. If necessary, select the **As independent graphic** option. Click **Open** or **OK**.
6. Position the loaded graphic icon on the pasteboard to the left of the document and click.
7. Drag the graphic to the left of the text that begins *Come join us*.
8. Save the publication as **Ex7-2** and leave it open for the next exercise.

❖ DRAWING SIMPLE GRAPHICS

PageMaker provides you with a set of tools to create your own simple graphics. The various drawing tools in the toolbox are identified in Figure 7–1.

When you select a drawing tool, a crossbar appears. To draw an object of an exact size or at an exact location, choose the appropriate tool and position the crossbar at what would be the uppermost left point of the object. Click and drag down and to the right. When you drag the tool, notice the dotted lines on the ruler moving to indicate your location on the page and the size of the object.

When you have completed drawing an object, sizing handles appear. Drag a handle to adjust the object's size. To move an object, select the Pointer tool and then click the object (not a handle) and drag to the desired location.

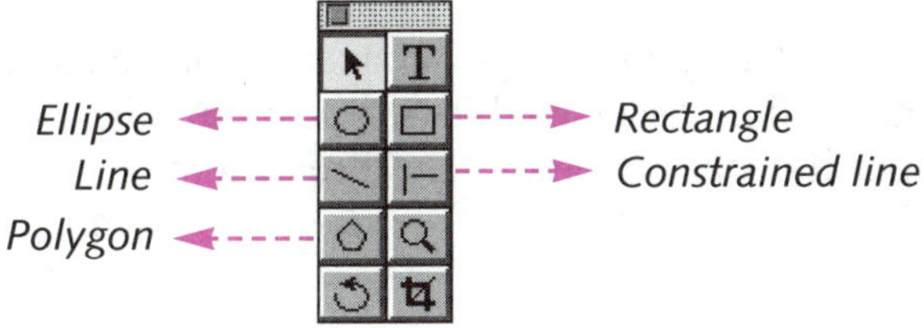

Figure 7–1 Drawing tools are used to create graphics.

RECTANGLES AND SQUARES

Use the Rectangle tool to draw rectangles or squares. To draw a perfect square, hold down the Shift key as you drag the crossbar.

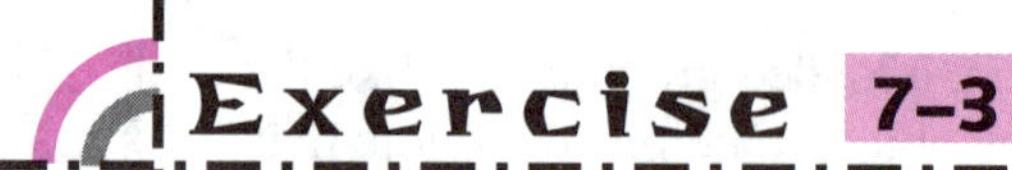

Draw a rectangle.

1. Select the **Rectangle** tool from the toolbox.
2. Draw a rectangle on the pasteboard that's approximately 1¾ inches wide by 2 inches high. Use the ruler to determine size. If necessary, drag the handles to adjust the size.
3. With the Pointer tool, click on a side (not a handle) of the rectangle and hold down the mouse button until the pointer turns into a four-headed arrow. Drag it to the lower right corner of the invitation.
4. Save the publication as **Ex7-3** and leave it open for the next exercise.

CIRCLES AND OVALS

Use the Ellipse tool to draw ovals and circles. To draw a perfect circle, hold down the Shift key as you drag the crossbar.

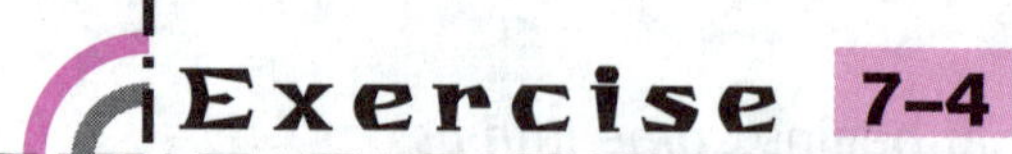

Draw a perfect circle.

1. Select the **Ellipse** tool. Hold down the **Shift** key and draw a circle on the pasteboard that is 2 inches wide by 2 inches high.
2. Place the circle beside the rectangle in the lower right corner of the invitation.
3. Save the publication as **Ex7-4** and leave it open for the next exercise.

POLYGONS

Use the Polygon tool to draw a five-sided polygon. You can change the number of sides on a polygon by using the Polygon Settings command on the Element menu.

The Polygon Settings dialog box appears, like that shown in Figure 7–2. You can designate the number of sides to be between 3 and 100. Enter the number in the text box or slide the box below it.

The Star inset option in the Polygon Settings dialog box lets you convert a polygon to a star shape with the same number of points as sides designated for the polygon. The higher the percentage of inset, the sharper the star becomes. The Preview box shows you what your figure will look like.

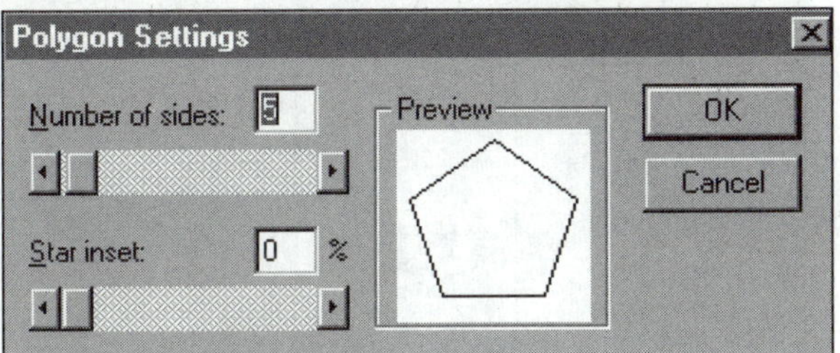

Figure 7–2
Specify the number of sides to a polygon in the Polygon Settings dialog box.

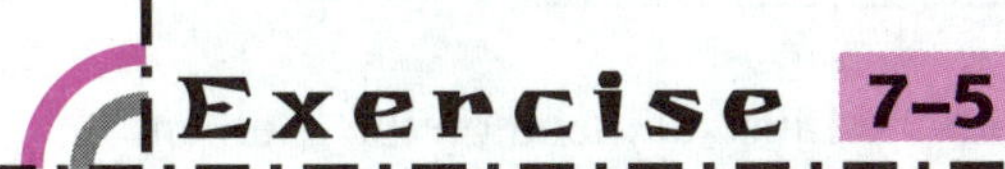

Exercise 7–5

Draw a star.

1. Select the **Polygon** tool and draw on the pasteboard a polygon of any size.
2. Select **Polygon Settings** on the Element menu. In the Polygon Settings dialog box, change the number of sides to **6.** Change the Star inset to **50%**. Click **OK**.
3. Reduce the size of the star to approximately ½-inch wide and ½-inch high using the handles.
4. Place the star within the circle at the bottom of the page.
5. Save the publication as **Ex7-5** and leave it open for the next exercise.

LINES

You can draw straight and angled lines with PageMaker's Line and Constrained-line tools. Use the Line tool to draw lines at any angle and the Constrained-line tool to draw straight lines at 45-degree and 90-degree angles.

Exercise 7–6

Draw lines in a publication.

1. Position the rectangle, circle, and star in the right corner of the page, as shown in Figure 7–3.
2. Use the **Line** tool to draw an angled line as shown in Figure 7–3.
3. Use the **Constrained-line** tool to draw a vertical straight line as shown in the figure.
4. If necessary, enlarge the view. Click the **Pointer** tool and move the map labels onto the diagram in the positions shown in Figure 7–3.
5. Save the publication as **Ex7-6** and leave it open for the next exercise.

❖ CHANGING THE LINE AND FILL

You can enhance the appearance of graphic objects, such as ovals, rectangles, and polygons, by changing the type and weight of their borders and by filling the objects

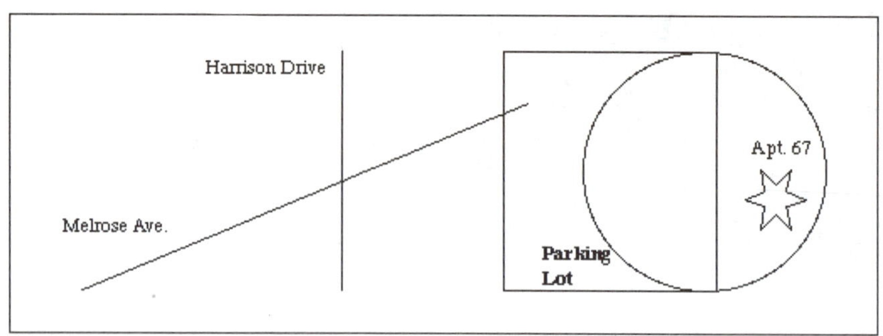

Figure 7–3
Drawing tools can be used to produce simple graphics.

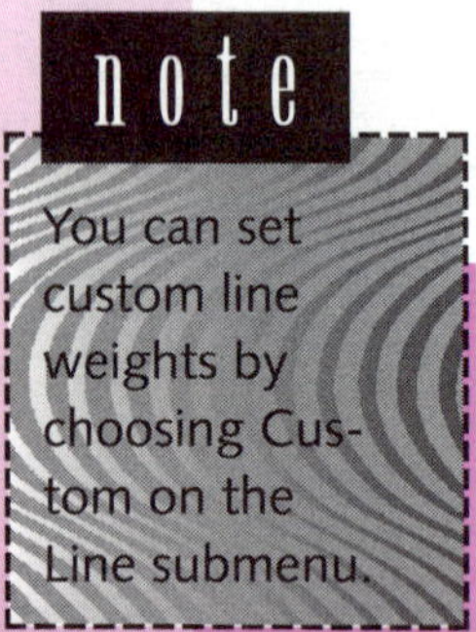

You can set custom line weights by choosing Custom on the Line submenu.

with patterns. You select line types and weights from the Line submenu on the Element menu, as shown in Figure 7–4. Reverse makes a line or border white.

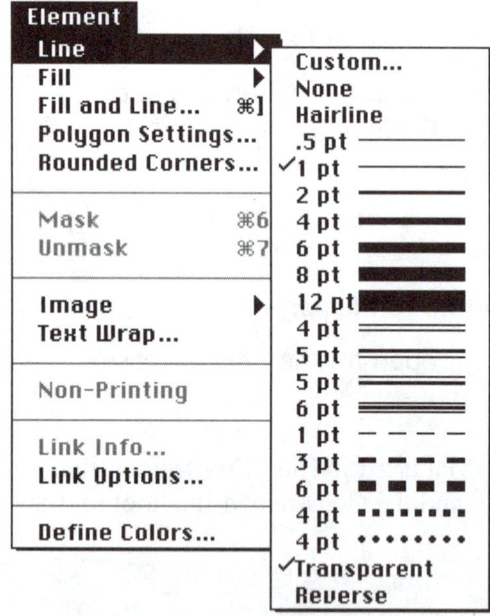

Figure 7–4
The Line submenu lists line types and weights.

To change the type or width of a line or border:

- Select the line or object.
- Choose **Line** on the Element menu.
- Choose the line style or weight that you want.

You can fill any object using the patterns in the Fill submenu on the Element menu, as shown in Figure 7–5. When None is selected, the object is transparent—that is, other objects show through it. When Paper fill is selected, objects "behind" it are hidden.

To change the fill:

- Select the object.
- Choose **Fill** on the Element menu. Fill and line patterns may vary slightly, depending on the printer used.
- Choose a fill pattern.

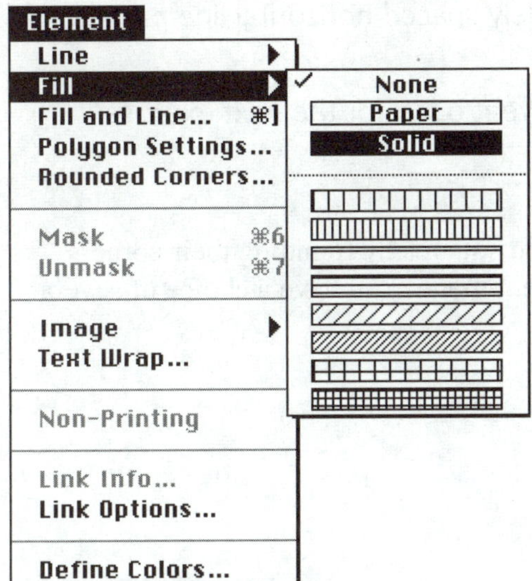

Figure 7–5
The Fill submenu shows different patterns.

You can change both the fill and line at the same time by selecting the Fill and Line command on the Element menu. The Fill and Line dialog box appears, as shown in Figure 7–6. Select the Fill pattern and Line width and type (and colors for each, if desired), and then click OK.

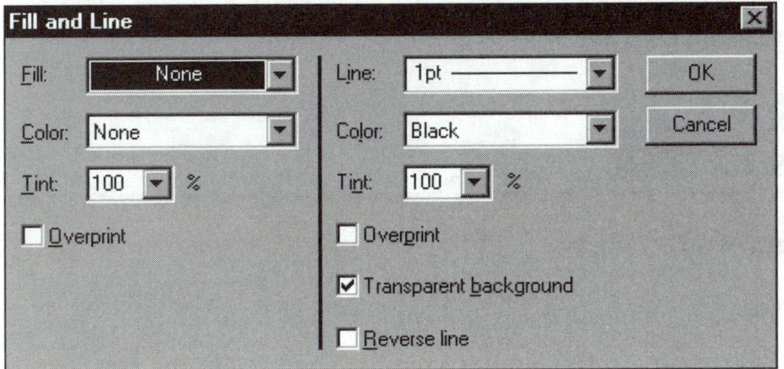

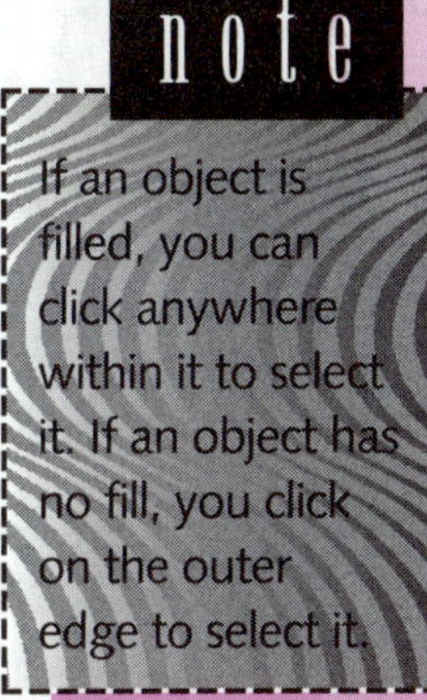

Figure 7–6
The Fill and Line dialog box allows you to change both the fill and the line type.

Exercise 7-7

Change the line weights and fill patterns.

1. Select the angled line for Melrose Ave. Select **Line** on the Element menu. Change the line to **12pt**.
2. Select the constrained line labeled Harrison Drive. Select **Line** on the Element menu. Change the line from a 1pt-single line to a **6pt**-multiple line.
3. Select the star. Select **Fill** on the Element menu and then select **Solid**.
4. Select the Circle. Fill it with **Paper**. You will learn how to redisplay the apartment number in a later exercise.

5. Select the rectangle. Fill it with the widely spaced horizontal line pattern. Change its border to **4pt**.
6. Save the publication as **Ex7-7** and leave it open for the next exercise.

❖ ROUNDING CORNERS

You can change the appearance of rectangles and squares by rounding their corners using the Rounded Corners option on the Element menu. You have a choice of several corner treatments, as shown in Figure 7–7.

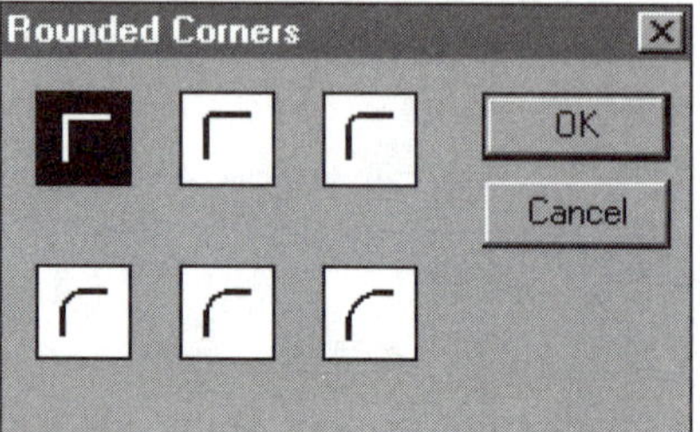

Figure 7–7 Rounding the corners of a rectangle gives you more drawing options.

To round the cornes of a rectangle or a square:

- Select the rectangle or square.
- Select **Rounded Corners** on the Element menu.
- Choose a corner style and click **OK**.

Exercise 7-8

Round the corners of a rectangle.

1. Select the rectangle.
2. Select **Rounded Corners** on the Element menu. Then select the last option in the second row. Click **OK**.
3. Save the publication as **Ex7-8** and leave it open for the next exercise.

❖ LAYERING OBJECTS

As items are created or imported into a publication, PageMaker gives them a stacking order from bottom to top in the order they were created or imported. You can rearrange the stacking order using the Bring to Front and Send to Back commands on the Arrange menu. These commands allow you to create interesting effects such as shadows and backgrounds for text.

The Bring to Front command brings the selected object to the top of the stack. The Send to Back command sends the selected object to the bottom of the stack. The Bring Forward and Send Backward commands on the Arrange menu move the selected object up or down one layer at a time.

Exercise 7–9

Change the stacking order of objects.

1. Select the circle. Select **Send to Back** on the Arrange menu.
2. Select the rectangle. Select **Send to Back** on the Arrange menu.
3. Select the **Melrose Ave. diagonal line** and send it to the back. Adjust the position of any labels, if necessary.
4. Save the publication as **Ex7-9** and leave it open for the next exercise.

❖ GROUPING AND UNGROUPING OBJECTS

Once objects have been imported or created, you may wish to group them so they can be handled as a single object. To group a series of objects, click the Pointer tool, hold down the mouse button, and drag the dotted box around the objects to be grouped. Select Group on the Arrange menu. To ungroup objects, select Ungroup on the Arrange menu.

❖ LOCKING PLACEMENT OF OBJECTS

Once an object or group of objects has been placed, you may want to lock it into that position to prevent accidental movement.

To lock the position of an object:

- Click the Pointer tool and select the object to be locked into place.
- Choose **Lock Position** on the Arrange menu.
- To unlock an object, select it and choose **Unlock** on the Arrange menu.

Exercise 7–10

Group objects and lock them in place.

1. Select the entire map at the bottom of the page by clicking the **Pointer** tool and dragging the dotted box around all the objects.
2. Choose **Group** on the Arrange menu.
3. Move the map so it is still at the bottom of the page but aligned at the left margin.
4. Choose **Lock Position** on the Arrange menu. If you try to move it now, you will be unable to.
5. Save the publication as **Ex7-10**.
6. Print the publication and then close it.

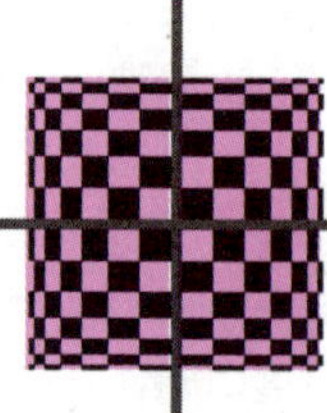

activities

❖ TRUE/FALSE

*On the blank line before each sentence, place a **T** if the statement is true and an **F** if it is false.*

____ 1. The toolbox contains the tools for drawing rectangles, polygons, ellipses, and lines.

____ 2. An inline graphic can be moved independently of text.

____ 3. The Ellipse tool lets you draw circles.

____ 4. The Constrained-line tool draws straight lines at any angle.

____ 5. PageMaker gives objects a stacking order from bottom to top in the order they were created or imported.

❖ COMPLETION

Answer the questions below in the space provided.

6. What purpose does the Line submenu serve?

____

____

7. How do you place an inline graphic?

____

____

8. How do you draw a perfect square?

____

____

9. What does a paper fill do?

____

____

10. What commands change the stacking order of objects?

____

____

Review Exercise 7-1

Manipulate graphic objects on a page.

1. Open **Truck** from the template files. You will see a number of filled shapes. Use them to create a drawing like that shown in Figure 7–8.
2. Copy and paste or draw any missing shapes. (Note that some colors/shading/patterns might appear differently on your screen than what's shown in the figure.)
3. Save the publication as **Re7-1**.
4. Print the publication, close it, and then end your PageMaker session.

Figure 7–8

Using Advanced Graphics Features

❖ OBJECTIVES

Upon completion of this lesson, you will be able to:

1. Use the Control Palette to enhance graphic objects.
2. Crop objects.
3. Resize objects.
4. Rotate objects.
5. Reflect objects.
6. Skew objects.
7. Wrap text around an object.
8. Mask objects

Estimated Time: 1 hour

❖ USING THE CONTROL PALETTE FOR OBJECTS

You have seen that the Control Palette offers you easier ways to format text and paragraphs. You can also use the Control Palette to modify graphic objects. When an object is selected, the Control Palette looks like Figure 8–1.

The Apply button is an icon indicating which tool was used to create the object. A box called a *proxy* also appears on the Control Palette. The proxy indicates handles on the object selected. The handle that is larger than the others is the *reference point*. The Control Palette displays information about an object based on the reference point setting on the proxy. For example, if the reference point setting for a rectangle is its upper left corner (the default), the X and Y options on the Control Palette display the position of the upper left corner of the rectangle relative to the rulers' zero point.

You can change the reference point by clicking on another handle in the proxy or on the object itself. Changes you make to objects with the Control Palette are affected by the reference point you set. The reference point can be an edge, a corner, or the center of a selected object.

note

If neither text nor an object is selected, the Control Palette displays the location of the tool selected. "X" indicates the tool's position in relation to the horizontal ruler and "Y" its position in relation to the vertical ruler.

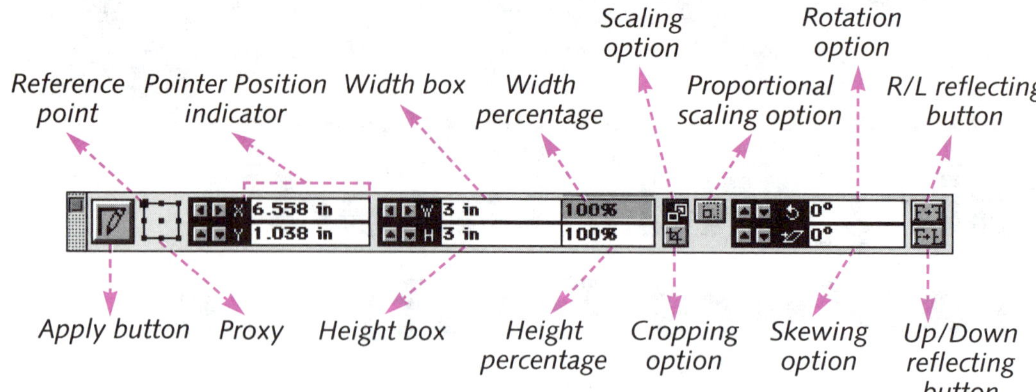

Figure 8–1
Use the Control Palette to modify graphic objects.

Exercise 8-1

Select an object and open the Control Palette.

1. Open **Overview** from the template files.
2. Click the computer graphic on the pasteboard.
3. Open the **Control Palette** on the Window menu.
4. Save the publication as **Ex8-1** to the folder or disk containing your course files and leave it open for the next exercise.

❖ CROPPING

Cropping a graphic lets you remove, or crop out, part of the graphic you don't want to appear on the page. You can crop using the Cropping option on the Control Palette or by using the Cropping tool in the Toolbox. Generally, it is easier to use the Cropping tool. Only imported graphics can be cropped.

If you crop a graphic and then change your mind, simply use the Cropping tool to pull out the handle along the side of the object that was cropped. While the portion of the graphic you cropped is removed from the page, the original object remains unchanged in the computer's memory.

To crop a graphic:

- Select the imported graphic with the **Cropping** tool.
- Click a handle on the side of the object that you want to crop and hold down the mouse button until a cropping box with a double-headed arrow appears.
- Drag the arrow to crop out the portion you want to remove.

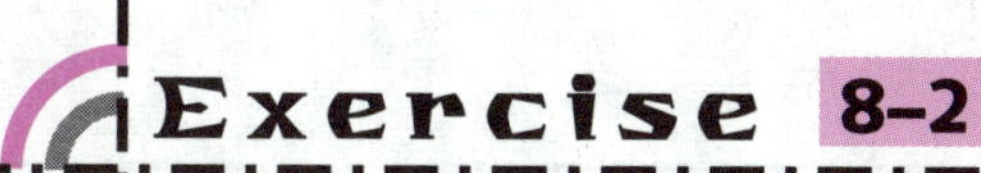

Exercise 8–2

Crop a graphic.

1. Import **Disk** from the template files:
   a. Select **Place** on the File menu.
   b. Select **Disk** and then click **As independent graphic**, if necessary.
   c. Click **Open** or **OK**.
   d. Position the loaded graphic cursor to the right of the page on the pasteboard and click.
2. Select the **Cropping** tool from the toolbox.
3. Click the handle at the lower right corner of the disk graphic, hold down the mouse button, and drag up and to the left to crop out the white space below and to the right of the disk.
4. Follow the same procedure to remove the white space on the top and left side. If part of the disk is accidentally cut off, use the Cropping tool to redisplay it.
5. Save the publication as **Ex8-2** and leave it open for the next exercise.

❖ RESIZING

You already know how to resize an object manually by dragging its handles using the Pointer tool. You can maintain the proportions by holding down the Shift key while dragging the handles.

You can also resize using the scaling options on the Control Palette. To maintain the proportions of the graphic, select the Proportional-scaling option. (See Figure 8–1.) Maintaining the proportions prevents distortion of your graphic.

To resize a graphic using the Control Palette:

- Select the graphic.
- Select a reference point on the proxy—usually the center. This ensures that the corresponding point on the actual object remains stationary as you modify the object.
- Select the **Proportional-scaling** option on the Control Palette.
- Key a new width or height into the width and height boxes, or key a new size percentage in the width or height percentage boxes. If one of the size boxes is grayed, click in the center of the proxy to change the reference point. It is not necessary to key a new percentage in both boxes if you have selected the Proportional-scaling option. PageMaker will automatically change the value in the other box.
- Press **Enter** (Windows) or **Return** (Macintosh).

note

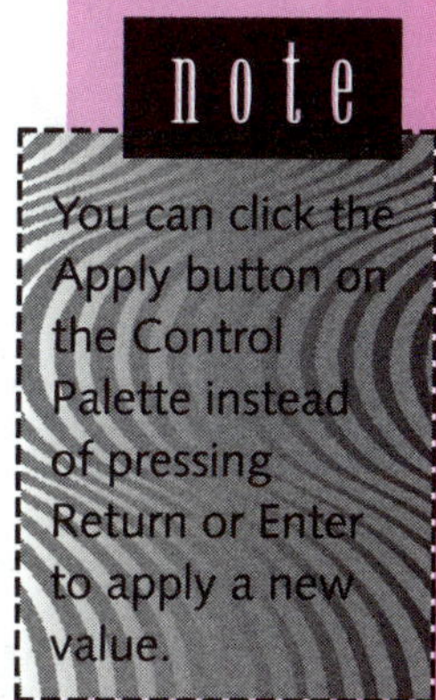

You can click the Apply button on the Control Palette instead of pressing Return or Enter to apply a new value.

Exercise 8-3

Resize a graphic proportionally.

1. Select the disk graphic with the **Pointer** tool.
2. On the proxy of the Control Palette, set the reference point in the middle of the object. Select the **Proportional-scaling** option on the Control Palette.
3. In the width percentage box, highlight **100%** and enter **25%**.
4. Click the **Apply** button.
5. Save the publication as **Ex8-3** and leave it open for the next exercise.

note

You can undo any changes you have made to an object using the Control Palette by rekeying the original value. If you are unsure how the changed object will look, record the original value so that you can return to it easily. You can also use the Undo command on the Edit menu.

❖ ROTATING

You can rotate objects up to 360 degrees left or right using the Rotation option on the Control Palette. (See Figure 8–1.) The rotating value is in degrees. To rotate an object, simply change the rotating value. You can also rotate an object manually using the Rotating tool in the Toolbox.

To rotate an object using the Rotation option on the Control Palette:

- Select the object.
- Select a reference point on the proxy (usually the center).
- Key a new rotation value in the Rotation box.
- Press **Enter** (Windows) or **Return** (Macintosh).

Exercise 8-4

Rotate a graphic.

1. **Copy** the disk graphic by selecting **Copy** on the Edit menu.
2. Select **Multiple Paste** on the Edit menu and enter **2** for the number of copies. Click **OK**.
3. Make sure one of the disk copies is selected. On the proxy, set the reference point at the center. On the Control Palette, highlight **0** in the Rotation box and key **45**. Click the **Apply** button.
4. Move the rotated copy of the disk so it is to the right of the headline.
5. Select the other copy of the disk. Change the rotation to **-45**. Click the **Apply** button.
6. Position the rotated disk to the left of the headline.
7. Save the publication as **Ex8-4** and leave it open for the next exercise.

❖ REFLECTING

Reflecting an object means to change its orientation by flipping it either vertically or horizontally to produce a mirrorlike image. Use the R/L Reflecting option on the Control Palette to flip objects right and left. Use the Up/Down Reflecting option to flip them up and down.

To reflect an object using the Control Palette:

- Select the object with the Pointer tool.
- Select a reference point (usually the center).
- Select a reflecting option on the Control Palette.
- Press **Enter** (Windows) or **Return** (Macintosh).

Exercise 8–5

Reflect a graphic.

1. Select the disk graphic on the pasteboard.
2. Click the **R/L Reflecting** option on the Control Palette.
3. Click the **Up/Down Reflecting** option.
4. Save the publication as **Ex8-5** and leave it open for the next exercise.

❖ SKEWING

When you want to slant, or *skew*, an object, you use the Skewing option on the Control Palette. (See Figure 8–1.) You can skew an object by as much as 85 degrees. Positive values move the top edge of the object to the right, and negative values move it to the left.

To skew an object using the Control Palette:

- Select the object with the Pointer tool.
- Select a reference point (usually the center).
- Key a skew angle in the Skewing box on the Control Palette.
- Press **Enter** (Windows) or **Return** (Macintosh).

Exercise 8–6

Skew a graphic.

1. Select the disk graphic on the pasteboard.
2. In the **Skewing** box on the Control Palette, highlight **0** and enter **25**. Click the **Apply** button.

3. Move the graphic to the bottom of the page below the last paragraph.
4. Save the publication as **Ex8-6** and leave it open for the next exercise.

❖ MASKING OBJECTS

Masking allows you to reveal only part of an object. The part that is not masked is obscured. You might want to use this feature to hide a portion of an object temporarily.

To mask an object or text block:

- Select the rectangle, ellipsis, or polygon tool in the Toolbox. This will serve as your mask.
- Using the selected tool, draw a graphic large enough to cover the object or portion of the object that you want to mask.
- Position the mask on top of the object you want to mask. (Remember that the object that is masked is the one that is revealed. Anything not masked is obscured.)
- Select both the mask and the object by dragging the Pointer tool around them to group them.
- Select **Group** on the Arrange menu.
- Select **Mask** on the Element menu.

To unmask an object or text block:

- Select the mask.
- Select **Unmask** on the Element menu.

Exercise 8–7

Mask a graphic.

1. Use the ellipsis tool to draw a circle or oval on the pasteboard approximately **2.5** inches in diameter. Notice that you can use the width and height options on the Control Palette to specify the exact dimensions once you have drawn the original circle.
2. Place the circle over the figure of the computer that's on the pasteboard. It's the one with the monitor.
3. Drag the Pointer tool around the circle and both computer graphics to group them.
4. Choose **Group** on the Arrange menu.
5. Choose **Mask** on the Element menu. The printer is obscured.
6. Save the publication as **Ex8-7** and leave it open for the next exercise.

❖ WRAPPING TEXT AROUND OBJECTS

In PageMaker publications, you can flow text around objects in a number of interesting ways.

To determine text flow, select the object and then select the Text Wrap command on the Element menu. The Text Wrap dialog box appears, as shown in Figure 8–2. Text can flow over, around, on either side of, or above and below an object. The Standoff measurement determines the amount of white space around a graphic.

Once you determine a Text Wrap option for a graphic, a boundary in the form of a dotted line appears around it on the page. Handles appear at each of the four corners. You can drag these handles to customize the flow of text around the graphic. You can also create additional handles on the boundaries by clicking anywhere along a boundary.

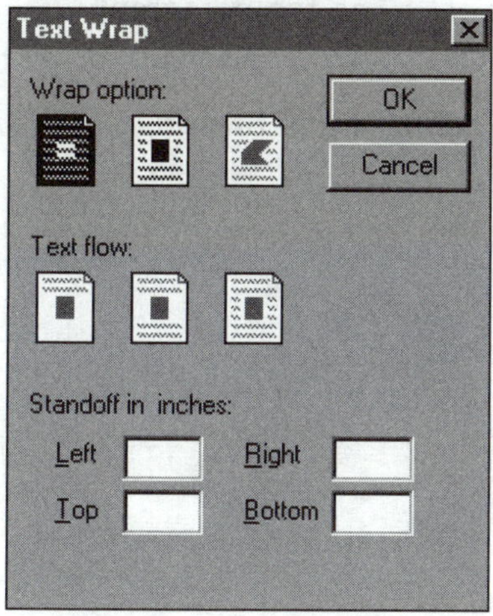

Figure 8–2
Text Wrap lets you choose the way text flows around graphics.

To wrap text around an object:

- Select the object with the Pointer tool.
- Choose **Text Wrap** on the Element menu.
- Click a Wrap option.
- Click a Text flow option.
- Enter the Standoff measurement.
- Click **OK**.

To customize the text wrap boundaries:

- Select the object with the Pointer tool.
- Click on a handle at one of the four corners of the dotted line.
- Drag the boundary to the new position.

To add handles to the text wrap boundaries:

- Select the object with the Pointer tool.
- Click on the dotted line to create a new handle.

Exercise 8-8

Use Text Wrap.

1. If necessary, select the masked computer graphic.
2. Choose **Text Wrap** on the Element menu.
3. Click on the middle wrap option. Use the default Text flow and Standoff settings.
4. Click **OK**.
5. Drag the computer graphic to the upper right corner of the publication just below the rotated disk graphic. (The printer graphic might reappear, but it will be obscured again once you position the object.) The top paragraph should flow around the graphic.
6. Delete the disk at the bottom of the page by selecting it and pressing **Delete**.
7. Save the publication as **Ex8-8**.
8. Print the publication and then close it.

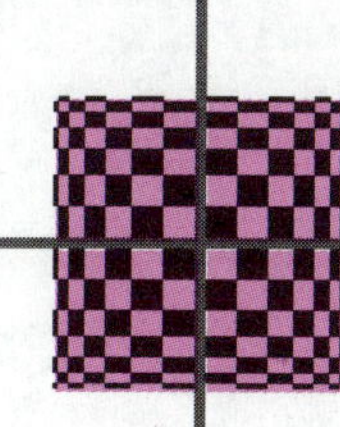

activities

❖ TRUE/FALSE

On the blank line before each sentence, place a **T** *if the statement is true and an* **F** *if it is false.*

____ 1. The Control Palette uses the proxy to determine size of an object.

____ 2. Skewing an object slants it left or right from the top edge.

____ 3. Cropping a graphic lets you remove portions of it.

____ 4. You can use the Reflecting tool to change the orientation of an object.

____ 5. When you wrap text around an object, the text can flow only to the right of the object.

❖ COMPLETION

Answer the questions below in the space provided.

6. What does the proxy indicate?

____

____

7. How is an object cropped?

____

____

8. What purpose does Masking serve?

____

____

9. What happens when you skew an object?

____

____

10. What purpose does the Standoff value serve in Text Wrap?

____

____

Review Exercise 8-1

Use advanced graphic features.

1. Open **Printers** from the template files.
2. Change the size of the body text to **18** point.
3. Create the publication shown in Figure 8–3 using the Control Palette:
   a. Rotate the subtitles 25 degrees.
   b. Reduce the subtitles 50%. (*Hint*: Use the **Proportional-scaling** option and enter **50%** in the Width percentage box.).
   c. Place the subtitles on the page as shown using the middle Text Wrap option and a **.1** Standoff measurement.
   d. Crop the computer (the object with the monitor) from the figure and then reflect the printer from right to left.
   e. Draw a box around the printer using a line type of your choice and then place it on the page.
4. Save the publication as **Re8-1**.
5. Print the publication, close it, and end your PageMaker session.

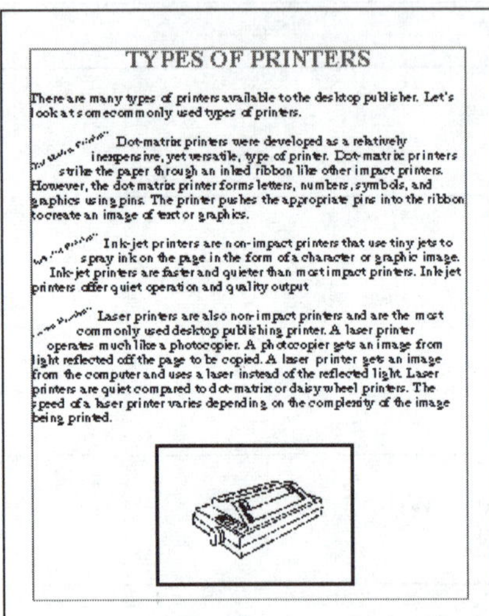

TYPES OF PRINTERS

There are many types of printers available to the desktop publisher. Let's look at some commonly used types of printers.

Dot-matrix printers were developed as a relatively inexpensive, yet versatile, type of printer. Dot-matrix printers strike the paper through an inked ribbon like other impact printers. However, the dot matrix printer forms letters, numbers, symbols, and graphics using pins. The printer pushes the appropriate pins into the ribbon to create an image of text or graphics.

Ink-jet printers are non-impact printers that use tiny jets to spray ink on the page in the form of a character or graphic image. Ink-jet printers are faster and quieter than most impact printers. Ink jet printers offer quiet operation and quality output

Laser printers are also non-impact printers and are the most commonly used desktop publishing printer. A laser printer operates much like a photocopier. A photocopier gets an image from light reflected off the page to be copied. A laser printer gets an image from the computer and uses a laser instead of the reflected light. Laser printers are quiet compared to dot-matrix or daisy wheel printers. The speed of a laser printer varies depending on the complexity of the image being printed.

Figure 8–3

Creating Layouts

❖ OBJECTIVES

Upon completion of this lesson, you will be able to:

1. Create appealing layouts.
2. Set up a new layout.
3. Insert and remove pages.
4. Set columns.
5. Flow text into columns.

Estimated Time: 1 hour

❖ CREATING AN APPEALING PAGE LAYOUT

The publications you create in PageMaker can range from simple to complex. Regardless of the design, though, you will work more efficiently if you determine the page layout before adding text or graphics. A page layout is a plan or set of guidelines for a page. Paper size, page orientation, number of pages, margin settings, columns, and the arrangement of columns on a page characterize the page layout.

The main objectives of a page design are readability and visual appeal. A publication with a well-designed page layout, such as the one shown in Figure 9–1, can motivate and entice the reader. The following guidelines help you create an appealing layout:

- Create asymmetrical layouts when possible; that is, page halves should not mirror each other.
- Enliven a publication with graphics that relate to the text.
- Be generous with the use of white space and avoid clutter.
- Use fonts creatively to make the publication more visually exciting, but don't overdo it. Limit yourself to two or three typefaces.
- Use boldface, italic, and underlining sparingly.

❖ SETTING UP A NEW LAYOUT

Layout decisions begin in the Document Setup dialog box, which appears after you choose New on the File menu. (See Figure 9–2.) So far, you have been using PageMaker's default settings to create new publications, but you can change options,

Lincoln High Times

Lincoln High Goes High Tech

The Lincoln High Times has traded its typewriter, lettering machine, and scissors for a computer and PageMaker desktop publishing software.

Greg Bussinger, a graduate of Lincoln High, donated a computer and laser printer to the journalism department. "I have felt indebted to the Lincoln High Journalism Department for the good experiences I had as an editor of the Lincoln High Times. I am happy to contribute to the school in this way," Bussinger said in a telephone interview with the Times.

In addition to its desktop publishing duties, the new computer will be used to keep track of yearbook orders this spring.

Yearbook Photographer Needed

Because of a recent increase in the number of school activities, the yearbook staff is seeking an additional photographer. Brandon Dobbs, head photographer, says that the new photographer must have his/her own 35 mm camera and must be enrolled in a photography or journalism class.

Lincoln Leopards Are Spotless

Not only are our Leopards one of only two undefeated football teams in our district this season, but the team is so serious about having a clean season that they have been called the "Spotless Leopards."

Coach Vince Maris told the Times that a renewed emphasis on sportsmanship has brought the teams closer together. "The team has done very well on the scoreboard so far this year. But I am particularly proud of the way the players handle themselves when they represent our school," Maris commented.

Maris said the true test of the team's attitude will be when Lincoln High meets its traditional rival, the Seamore Skunks, next week.

Figure 9–1
A well-designed newsletter makes use of a multicolumn layout and white space.

Document Setup

Page size: Letter
Dimensions: 8.5 x 11 inches
Orientation: Tall Wide
Options: Double-sided
Facing pages
Restart page numbering
Number of pages: 1 Start page #: 1
Margins
Inside: 1 inches Outside: 0.75 inches
Top: 0.75 inches Bottom: 0.75 inches
Target printer resolution: 300 dpi
Compose to printer: HP LaserJet Series II on \\Cep_1\hp
OK
Cancel
Numbers...

Figure 9–2
Set page layout options in the Document Setup dialog box.

such as page size, page orientation, page numbering, and margins by selecting them in the Document Setup dialog box.

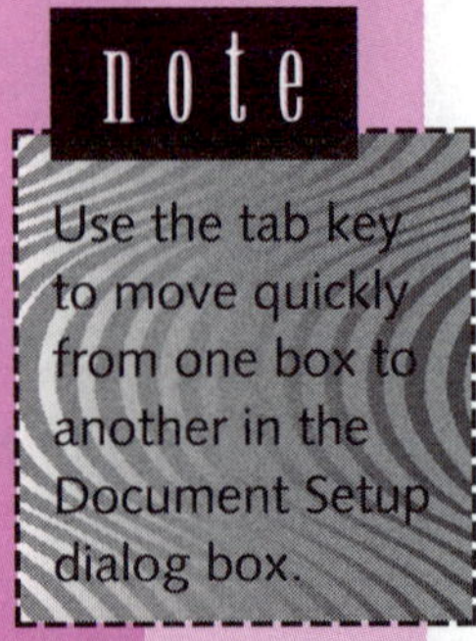

PAGE SIZE AND DIMENSIONS

Among the most common page sizes to choose from are letter, legal, and tabloid. A standard sheet of paper commonly used for form letters measures 8.5 × 11 inches; the size of legal paper is 8.5 × 14 inches. Tabloid paper is 11 × 14 inches. Tabloid-size paper is also called *ledger paper.* Letterhalf and Legalhalf sizes are half the size of letter and legal paper. These sizes can be used for creating a folded booklet. You can also create a custom page size by keying in specific page dimensions.

ORIENTATION

You select either Tall or Wide as the orientation of a publication. *Orientation* refers to the vertical or horizontal position of the page. With Tall orientation, the page appears taller than it is wide. This is sometimes referred to as *portrait.* With Wide orientation, the page appears wider than it is tall. This is sometimes called *landscape orientation.*

OPTIONS

To view pages that face each other when printed, choose Double-sided and Facing pages in the Document Setup dialog box. This helps you design a layout that is attractive to the reader, who sees the open pages as a single unit.

NUMBER OF PAGES

You can determine the number of pages in your document in the Document Setup dialog box. If you don't know the number of pages, you can easily add and remove pages as you work on your publication. You also can determine on which page you would like page numbering to start.

MARGINS

When setting your margins, remember to allow space on the side that will be bound. The default setting allows an additional quarter inch on the left side.

> **note**
>
> Once a publication has been created, you can change the layout options at any time by choosing Document Setup on the File menu.

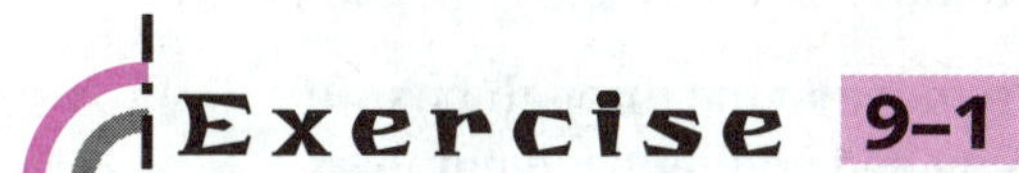

Exercise 9-1

Set layout options for a publication.

1. Create a new publication by selecting **New** on the File menu. In the Document Setup dialog box:
   a. Change the page size to **Legal** and the orientation to **Wide**.
   b. If necessary, set the Options for **Double-sided** and **Facing pages**.
   c. Change the Number of pages to **3** and the Start page # to **2**.
   d. Change the Margins to **2** inches on the Inside, Outside, Top, and Bottom.
2. Click **OK**. Notice in the bottom left corner that there are three page icons, beginning with the number 2.
3. Save the publication as **Ex9-1** and leave it open for the next exercise.

❖ INSERTING AND REMOVING PAGES

The number of pages in a publication is set when you first create a new publication, but pages can be added or deleted as needed. If you delete, be careful that you do not remove a page that contains text or graphics you want to keep. If you accidentally delete a page, you can restore it by immediately selecting the Undo command on the Edit menu.

To insert a new page:

- Select **Insert Pages** on the Layout menu. The Insert Pages dialog box appears, as shown in Figure 9–3.
- Key the number of pages you want to insert.
- Click the current page arrow to choose the location of the new pages. They may be placed before, after, or between current pages.
- Click **Insert**.

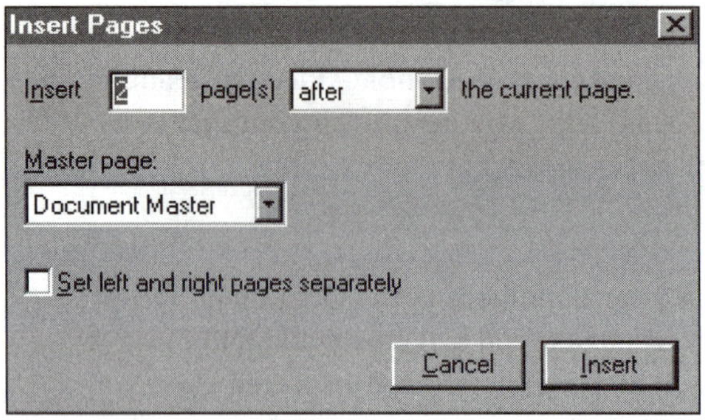

Figure 9–3
The Insert Pages dialog box automatically defaults to 2 pages.

To remove a page:

- Choose **Remove Pages** on the Layout menu. The Remove Pages dialog box appears, as shown in Figure 9–4.
- Key the number of the first page you want to remove in the Remove page(s) box.
- Key the number of the last page you want to remove in the through box. If you want to remove a single page, the beginning and ending page numbers are the same.
- Click **OK**.

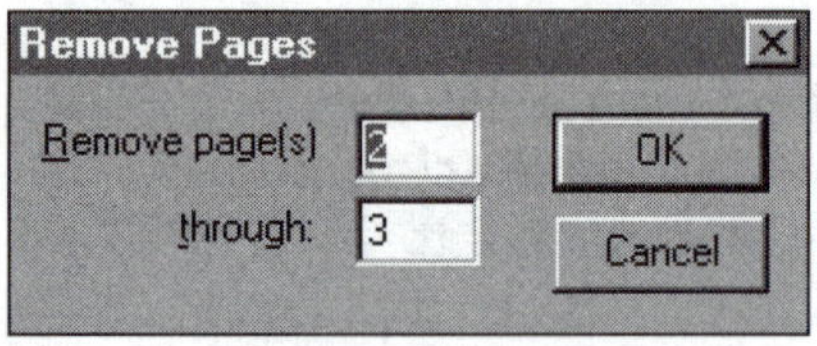

Figure 9–4
The Remove Pages dialog box defaults to the pages that are currently on the screen.

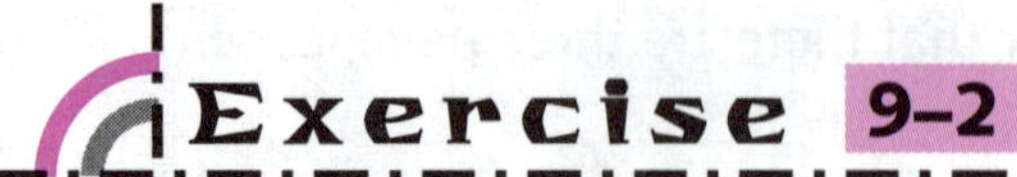

Exercise 9–2

Insert and remove pages.

1. Select **Insert Pages** on the Layout menu. Key **3** in the Insert page(s) box. Select **before** in the current page box. Click **Insert**.
2. Select **Document Setup** on the File menu and change the Page size to **Letter**. You might have to scroll to see the Letter option. Your margins change to the default values.
3. Change the margins to **1** inch. Click **OK**.
4. Select **Remove Pages** on the Layout menu and remove pages **4** through **7** from your publication. A message box appears, warning you that you will remove the pages and their contents. Click **OK**.
5. Save the publication as **Ex9-2** and leave it open for the next exercise.

❖ SETTING COLUMNS

PageMaker lets you create publications with up to 20 columns per page. You might want to limit the number of columns on a page so that they are wide enough to fit at least five words on a line. Columns are designated by double vertical lines called *column guides*. These lines do not print.

To set the number of columns on a page:

- Choose **Column Guides** on the Layout menu. The Column Guides dialog box appears, as shown in Figure 9–5. Notice the default settings.
- To change the default setting, key a number in the Number of columns box.
- In the Space between columns box, enter the amount of space in inches.
- If you have facing pages and want to set different columns for each page, click on **Set left and right pages separately**.
- Choose **OK**.

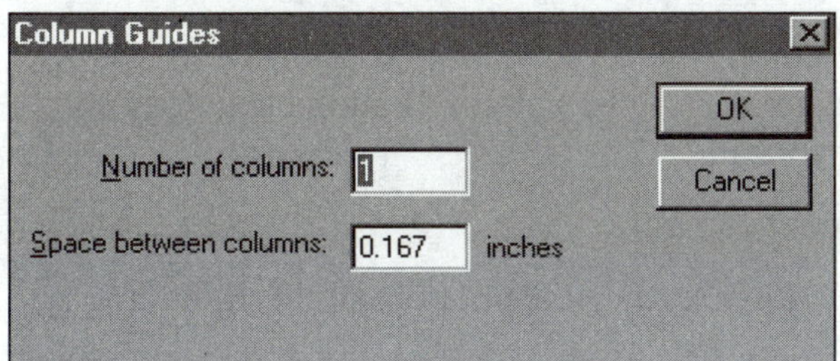

Figure 9–5
The Column Guides dialog box uses 0.167 inches as the default space between columns.

To change the width of a column:

- Select the Pointer tool. Click on one of the column guides on the page and hold down the mouse button. The Pointer tool turns into a double-sided arrow.
- Drag the column guide to a new location to change the column width. Both guides move at once, maintaining the space between columns. The position of the column guide is indicated on the ruler.

Set page columns.

1. Choose **Column Guides** on the Layout menu.
2. Click the option to **Set left and right pages separately**.
3. Key **3** columns on the Left page and **2** columns on the Right page.
4. Set the Space between columns on both sides at **.5** inches. Click **OK**.
5. With the Pointer tool, click on the column guide on Page 3 and hold down the mouse button. Drag the column guide to the **5**-inch mark.
6. Save the publication as **Ex9-3** and leave it open for the next exercise.

❖ FLOWING TEXT INTO COLUMNS

Once a layout has been set, text and graphics can be placed on the page. Text can be “poured” or flowed into columns manually, one column at a time, or continuously using the Autoflow command. Text that flows from one column to another is linked so that any change in one column repositions the text in all linked columns.

Once text has been flowed into a column, the width of the text block is maintained even if you change the width of the column. To change the width of the text block, you have to use the handles of the text block to change its size or reflow the column.

It is not necessary to click exactly on the left margin of the column to have text fill the column. However, if you want to ensure that text flows from the top of the column, you must click at the top. If necessary, you may drag the text block to the top of the column after the text flows into the column.

To flow imported text into a single column:

- Choose **Place** on the File menu.
- In the Place dialog box, select the file you want to place. Click **Open** or **OK**.
- Click the loaded text icon in the column where you want to begin flowing the text. Text flows down the column and stops at the bottom. If all the text does not fit into the column, a down arrow appears.

To flow text from one column into the next column:

- Use the Pointer tool to click on the down arrow at the bottom of the column. The text icon appears.
- Click in the next column. Text again flows down the column and stops. If all the text does not fit into the column, another down arrow appears.

To reflow text into a column:

- Use the Pointer tool to click on the icon at the bottom of the column and drag up until all the text disappears. When you release the mouse button, the down arrow is visible.
- Click on the down arrow. The text icon appears.
- Click in a new column. Text reflows down the column.

To flow text continuously using the Autoflow command:

- Choose **Autoflow** on the Layout menu.
- Choose **Place** on the File menu.
- Select the file you want to place.
- An Autoflow text icon appears. Click in the first column where you want to begin flowing the text. Text flows down the column and continues to each succeeding column. If additional pages are needed, the Autoflow command creates new pages until all text is placed.

To Autoflow text from a column of text already placed:

- Choose **Autoflow** on the Layout menu.
- Use the Pointer tool to click on the down arrow at the bottom of the column. The Autoflow text icon appears.
- Click in the next column. Text flows down the column and continues on to each succeeding column.

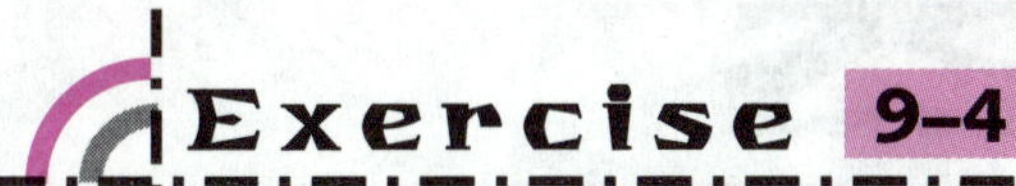

Exercise 9–4

Flow text into columns.

1. Select **Place** on the File menu. From the template files, select **Format**. Click **Open**. A text icon appears.
2. Click at the top of the first column on Page 2. Text flows down the column and stops. Click on the down arrow that appears at the bottom of the column. A text icon appears. Click at the top of the second column on Page 2. Continue until all the text is placed.
3. On Page 3, drag the left column guide to the **3**-inch mark. The size of the text block remains unchanged.
4. On Page 3, drag the bottom handle of the text block in the right column up to the top of the column. The text disappears. Do the same to the text in the left column on Page 3.
5. Choose **Autoflow** on the Layout menu.
6. Click the text block in column 3 of Page 2, and then click the down arrow at the bottom of the column.
7. Click the Autoflow text icon at the top of the left column on Page 3. The text reflows into the new columns.
8. On Page 2, drag the bottom handle on the middle column up above the word *Orientation*. It is bumped up to the top of the next column.
9. If necessary, move the text block in column 3 of Page 2 up so the word *Orientation* is flush with the top margin. Drag the bottom handle down to extend the text to the bottom margin.
10. Save the publication as **Ex9-4**.
11. Print the publication and then close it.

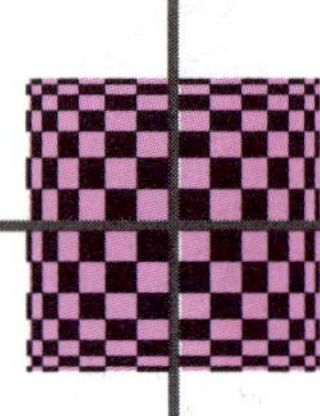

activities

❖ TRUE/FALSE

On the blank line before each sentence, place a **T** *if the statement is true and an* **F** *if it is false.*

____ 1. The main objective of a good layout is to place as much text on a page as possible.

____ 2. Orientation of a page can be either tall or wide.

____ 3. The document setup cannot be changed once the new publication has appeared on the screen.

____ 4. PageMaker limits to five the number of columns you can place on a page.

____ 5. You can flow text manually, column by column, or continuously, using the Autoflow command.

❖ COMPLETION

Answer the questions below in the space provided.

6. What are at least two ways to add readability and visual appeal to a layout?

____

____

7. What layout options can you select in the Document Setup dialog box?

____

____

8. Why would you want to see facing pages?

____

____

9. What would happen if you removed a page that contained text or graphics?

____

____

10. What is the purpose of the Autoflow command?

____

____

Review Exercise 9-1

Create and enhance a layout.

1. Open **InfoTech** from the template files. Text and graphic objects have been placed on the pasteboard. You may need to scroll to see them.
2. Create a layout like the one shown in Figure 9–6. Use the tools and features you have learned thus far in the course.
3. Save the publication as **Re9-1**.
4. Print the publication and then close it.

INFO TECH

DESKTOP PUBLISHING TECHNOLOGY

HARDWARE

Microprocessor

Memory

Disk Storage

PRINTERS

SOFTWARE

CONCLUSION

Figure 9–6

Review Exercise 9-2

Design a poster.

1. Open **Poster** from the template files.
2. Use the text and any of the graphic objects on the pasteboard to create an attractive layout for a one-page informational poster. Change fonts, type styles, sizes, columns, or spacing to improve readability. Remember that you can use cropping, sizing, and text wrap tools to enhance your design.
3. Save the publication as **Re9-2**.
4. Print the publication, close it, and end your PageMaker session.

Creating an Advanced Publication Design

❖ OBJECTIVES

Upon completion of this lesson, you will be able to:

1. Place secondary margin guides.
2. Use ruler guides.
3. Use snap to rulers and guides.
4. Lock guides.
5. Change ruler settings.

Estimated Time: 1/2 hour

❖ INTRODUCTION

PageMaker provides you with a number of alignment tools to help you create professional-looking documents. In the previous lesson, you learned how to set up column guides on a page into which you flowed text. In this lesson, you will learn how to use other guides and rulers to design your page.

❖ USING MARGIN GUIDES

You already know how to set margins using the Document Setup dialog box. These margins are set for every page in your publication, but you can change the margins on individual pages by pulling secondary margins from the side page margins.

Once the new margin guides are dragged into place, text can be flowed between them rather than between the original margins (see Figure 10–1). Thus, you can set up margins in the Document Setup dialog box and then use the secondary margin guides to change the margins on individual pages.

To create a secondary margin guide:

- With the Pointer tool, click the vertical margin on the left or right side of the screen to grab a secondary margin. Hold down the mouse button until the Pointer tool turns into a double-headed arrow.
- Drag the secondary margin into position.

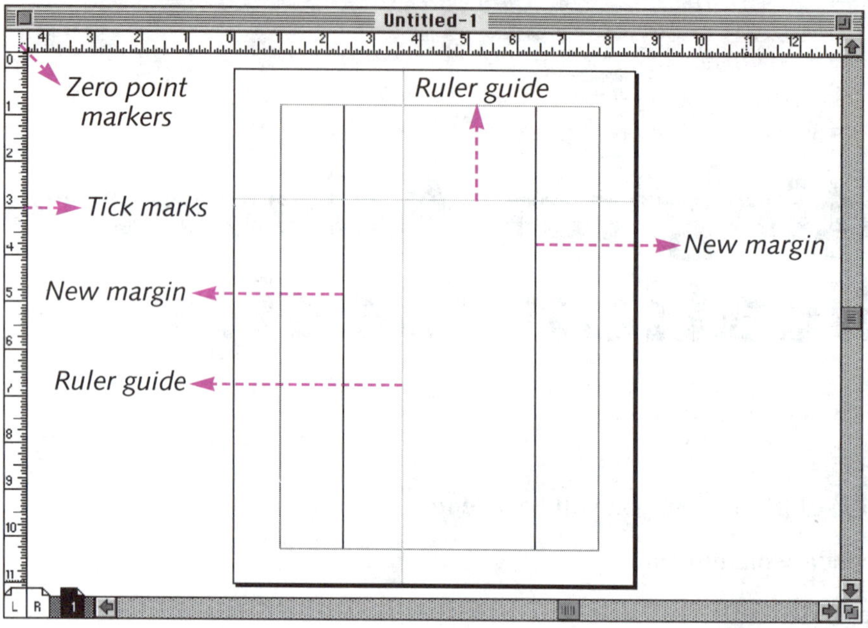

Figure 10–1 Ruler guides and secondary margin guides increase your layout options.

note

If you are working on a color monitor, you might have noticed that the side margins are a different color than the top margins. PageMaker frequently uses color changes to indicate alignment. Once you have pulled away the secondary margin, the side margin becomes the same color as the top. If you remove the secondary margin, the permanent margin changes color to indicate alignment.

To remove a secondary vertical margin guide:

- With the Pointer tool, click the secondary margin and hold down the mouse button.
- Drag the secondary margin off the page.

Exercise 10–1

Set secondary margins.

1. Open **Paint** from the template files. If necessary, maximize the window.
2. Position the Pointer tool on the left margin, click, and hold down the mouse button. When it turns into a doubled-headed arrow, drag the secondary margin to the **4.25**-inch mark on the ruler.
3. Change the page view to **Actual Size**. If necessary, adjust the margin to the specified measurement.
4. Save the publication as **Ex10-1** to the disk or folder containing your course files and leave it open for the next exercise.

❖ USING RULER GUIDES

Ruler guides can help you align objects on your pages. As shown in Figure 10–1, ruler guides are vertical and horizontal lines that extend from the tick marks of the rulers. *Tick marks* are the division lines on a ruler.

To create a vertical or horizontal ruler guide:

- With the Pointer tool, click on the vertical or horizontal ruler to grab a guide and hold down the mouse button.
- When the Pointer tool turns into a double-headed arrow, drag the guide into position. You can drag up to 40 ruler guides onto the page.
- To remove a ruler guide, simply drag it off the page.

note

Ruler lines and guide lines used in PageMaker are visible on the screen, but they do not appear on the printed page.

Exercise 10–2

Place vertical and horizontal ruler guides.

1. Change the page view to **Fit in Window**.
2. Click on the vertical ruler. When the pointer turns into a double-headed arrow, drag a ruler guide to the **1.5**-inch mark. Drag another to the **4**-inch mark.
3. Drag guides from the horizontal ruler to the **1**-inch and **4**-inch marks.
4. Change the page view to **Actual Size**. If necessary, adjust the guides to the specified measurements.
5. Save the publication as **Ex10-2** and leave it open for the next exercise.

SELECTING SNAP TO RULERS AND GUIDES

You might have noticed as you placed text and objects on a page that they automatically aligned themselves with a margin guide. This feature was designed to eliminate the sometimes tedious task of aligning objects precisely on your pages. In fact, PageMaker lets you "snap" objects into place on margin guides and on ruler guides.

To turn the features on or off, select Snap to Rulers (aligns object with the nearest ruler guide or tick mark) or Snap to Guides (aligns objects with the nearest margin guide) from the Guides and Rulers option on the Layout menu, as shown in Figure 10–2. When the features are on, a check mark appears beside them on the menu.

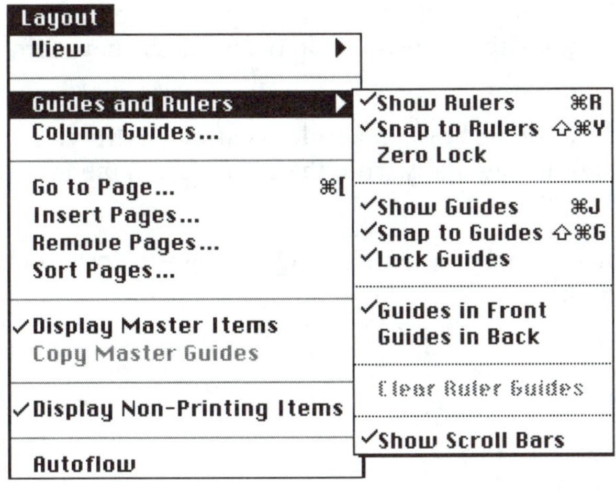

Figure 10–2
Snap to options speed up placement and ensure more accurate positioning of objects on a page.

Another handy alignment feature is the Lock Guides option on the Guides and Rulers submenu. Turning on this option lets you lock a secondary margin or ruler guide into place. This prevents you from inadvertently moving a guide as you position objects on a layout.

Another feature on the Guides and Rulers submenu is the Show Rulers and Show Guides options. If Show Guides is checkmarked, the guides are visible. If Show Rulers is checkmarked, the rulers are visible. Toggling to remove the check marks removes the rulers and guides from the screen. This is useful if you want to see what your publication looks like without the distractions of nonprinting lines.

Exercise 10–3

Align objects using the Snap to and Lock Guides options.

1. Change the view to **Fit in Window**.
2. Choose **Guides and Rulers** on the Layout menu. Make sure that **Snap to Guides** is on. It should have a check mark beside it.
3. Choose **Guides and Rulers** again. Turn on the **Lock Guides** option.
4. Drag the artist's palette graphic to the top rectangle you formed with the ruler guides. (*Hint:* The top left corner of the rectangle is at the 1.5-inch mark on the horizontal ruler and the 1-inch mark on the vertical ruler.)
5. Choose **Guides and Rulers**. Toggle off the **Show Rulers** and **Show Guides** options.
6. Save the publication as **Ex10-3** and leave it open for the next exercise.

❖ CHANGING RULER SETTINGS

PageMaker allows you to change the ruler settings on both the horizontal and vertical rulers and then to lock the new settings in place. This is helpful when you want to measure from a specific point, such as the center of the page.

As shown in Figure 10–1, in the upper left corner of the publication page where the rulers meet, there is a box with intersecting dotted lines called the *zero-point marker.* You use the Pointer tool to grab these lines and drag them to a new spot on the rulers. When you release the mouse button, the point at which you stop becomes the new zero point on the ruler.

If you move horizontally along the ruler, only the horizontal ruler is affected. Moving vertically changes the vertical ruler. Moving diagonally from the upper left to the lower right changes both rulers.

Once a new ruler setting is in place, you can lock the setting by choosing the Zero Lock option on the Guides and Rulers submenu.

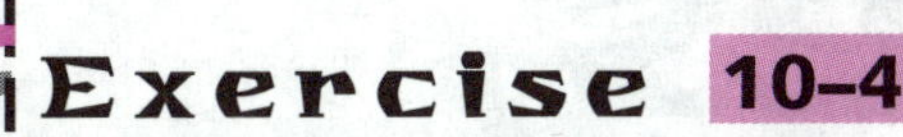

Set and lock new zero points.

1. Choose **Guides and Rulers** on the Layout menu. Toggle on the **Show Rulers** and **Show Guides** options.
2. Use the Pointer tool to grab the horizontal zero point marker. Drag the marker to the 1.5-inch mark on the vertical ruler.
3. Use the Pointer tool to grab the vertical zero point marker. Drag the marker to the 1-inch mark on the horizontal ruler.
4. Choose **Guides and Rulers**. Click **Zero Lock** to lock the new ruler settings in place.
5. Save the publication as **Ex10-4**.
6. Print the publication and then close it.

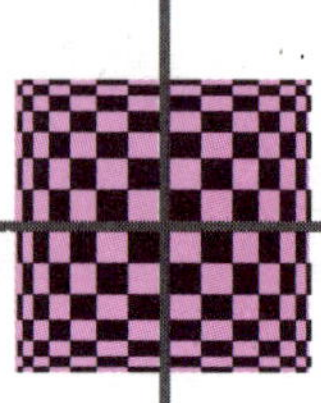

activities

❖ TRUE/FALSE

On the blank line before each sentence, place a T if the statement is true and an F if it is false.

____ 1. Secondary margin guides can be different on every page.

____ 2. You can have only one set of ruler guides on a page.

____ 3. Snap to Guides are useful to improve the accuracy of the placement of an object.

____ 4. Zero point markers can be moved to change the ruler settings.

____ 5. Hiding guides ensures that they will not print.

❖ COMPLETION

Answer the questions below in the space provided.

6. Why would you lock the guides of a publication?

____

____

7. Once new secondary margin guides are in place, how does text flow?

____

____

8. When does a margin change color?

____

____

9. What does a check mark indicate next to the Snap to Rulers option?

____

____

10. When would you want to change a zero point?

____

____

Review Exercise 10-1

Set guides on a page.

1. Open **Multi** from the template files.
2. Make sure the **Snap to Guides** and **Snap to Rulers** options are on.
3. If necessary, set the zero point markers at the the **.75**-inch mark on both the horizontal and vertical rulers.
4. Drag secondary vertical page margins to **1** inch and **6** inches.
5. Using the horizontal ruler guides, place guides at the **6.25**-, **5.75**-, **1.75**-, and **1.25**-inch marks.
6. Using the vertical ruler guides, place guides at the **4.75**-, **4.5**-, **2.5**-, and **2.25**-inch marks.
7. Turn on the **Lock Guides** option.
8. Move the text block (not the text block with the title) on the pasteboard into area 1 as shown in Figure 10–3. Resize the text block to fit within the secondary margins.
9. Click the arrow in the windowshade handle and continue the story in area 2, area 3, and area 4. Adjust the text blocks as shown.
10. Move the title text block from the pasteboard to the page as shown.

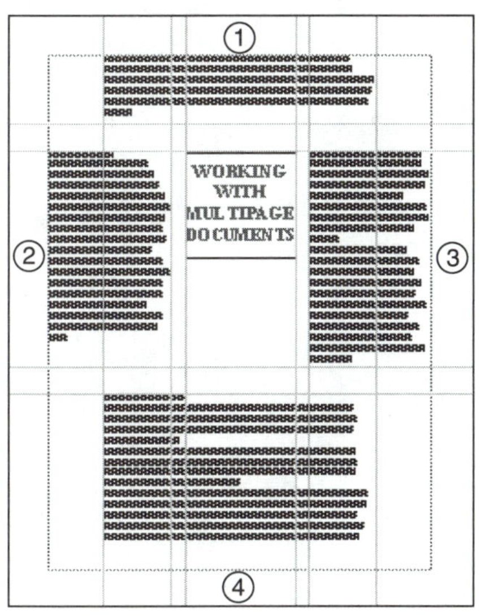

Figure 10–3

11. Highlight the title. Turn off hyphenation and center it. (*Hint:* The **Hyphenation** and **Alignment** options are on the Type menu.)

12. Place a 2-point black rule above the paragraph and one below it. (*Hint:* Select **Paragraph** on the Type menu.) Then click **Rules**. Select the **2pt** Line style for the rule above and below the paragraphs. Click **Options** and place the rule **.5** inches above the baseline and **.3** inches below the baseline.

13. Return to the publication and save it as **Re10-1**.

14. Print the publication, close it, and end your PageMaker session.

Using Shortcuts

❖ OBJECTIVES

Upon completion of this lesson, you will be able to:

1. Create master pages.
2. Add master pages.
3. Define and apply styles.
4. Set up a Library Palette.
5. Use the Colors Palette.

Estimated Time: 1 hour

❖ CREATING MASTER PAGES

Master pages can be a real time saver when you want to create publications that contain recurring layouts, text, or graphics. Master page icons are located to the left of the numbered page icons that appear at the bottom of your page when a file is open (see Figure 11–1).

The page icon labeled L (for left) represents pages on the left of a two-page spread, or those that are even numbered. The icon labeled R represents all pages on the right of a two-page spread, or those that are odd numbered. Note in Figure 11–1 that there are three numbered page icons, which means that the document contains three pages. To go to a master page or to a numbered page, simply click the appropriate page icon and it becomes highlighted. When you click on a page that is part of a two-page spread (such as page 2 in Figure 11–1), both pages in the spread appear on your screen.

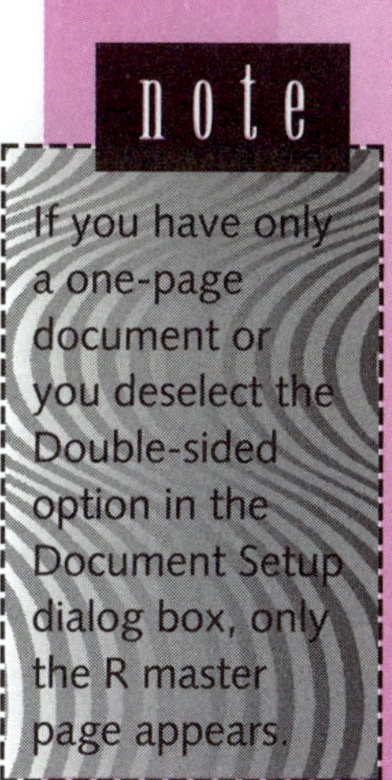

When you want an object, such as a text block or graphic, to appear on every page in your publication, you have to add it only once to the master pages. You can also set columns, ruler guides, and secondary margins on master pages.

For example, you might want a header or footer that lists the name of the publication or a date to appear on each page. You might also want each page to have three columns. Instead of entering this information and setting the number of columns on each page, you simply click on a master page icon and then set the number of columns and enter the information in the position you want it to appear. The object then appears in the same position, and three columns appear on each page in the publication. You can set master items on either the left or right master page, or both.

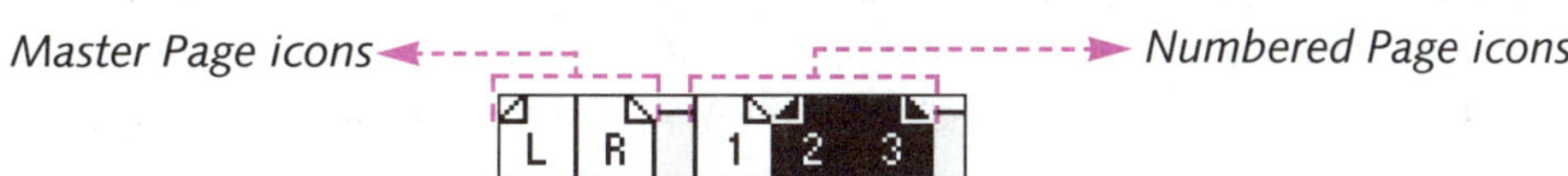

Figure 11–1
Master page icons are identified with an R and L for right and left.

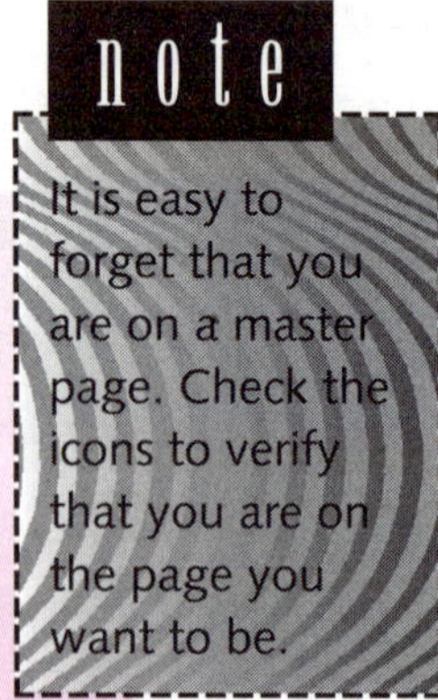

Frequently, you'll want the pages in your publication to be numbered. This is accomplished easily by setting them on master pages. To number pages automatically, press CTRL + Shift + 3 (Windows) or Command + Option + P (Macintosh). A page number marker LM (left page marker) or RM (right page marker) appears. The markers are readable when your view of the page is enlarged. The numbers on the pages match the number of the page icon.

If you do not want master objects to appear on a page, deselect Display Master Items on the Layout menu or move or delete the objects individually.

If you make a change to the master items on a page and decide you want to return to the original master page settings, choose Copy Master Guides on the Layout menu. Your changes to the page are replaced by the master page settings.

Exercise 11-1

Create a master page.

1. Open **Memo** from the template files.
2. Click the **R** master page icon.
3. Choose **Column Guides** on the Layout menu and enter **2** for the Number of columns with **.3** inches of space between columns. Click **OK**.
4. Click and drag the column guide so it lines up at the 3-inch mark on the ruler.
5. Pull down a horizontal ruler guide to the 3-inch mark.
6. With the Text tool, key **Copper H.S. Memo** anywhere on the page.
7. Tab once. Key **Page**, press the **spacebar**, and press **CTRL + Shift + 3** (Windows) or **Command + Option + P** (Macintosh) to automatically number the pages.
8. Highlight the text and select **Align Right** on the Alignment submenu on the Type menu.
9. Place the text block below the bottom page margin and enlarge the block so it is as wide as the page margins. This is the footer that will appear on all pages in your publication.
10. Click the **page 1 icon**. You should see the new footer, horizontal ruler guide, and columns on the page.
11. Save the publication as **Ex11-1** to the folder or disk containing your course files and leave it open for the next exercise.

❖ CREATING ADDITIONAL MASTER PAGES

By default, each new publication includes a Document Master that is applied to the pages. The options you specify in the Document Setup dialog box determine the margins, orientation, and so on, of the Document Master. You can create additional master pages that apply to individual pages. This allows you to further customize pages.

To create a new master page:

- Select **Master Pages** on the Window menu. A Master Pages palette appears, like that shown in Figure 11–2. It lists the names of all current master pages.

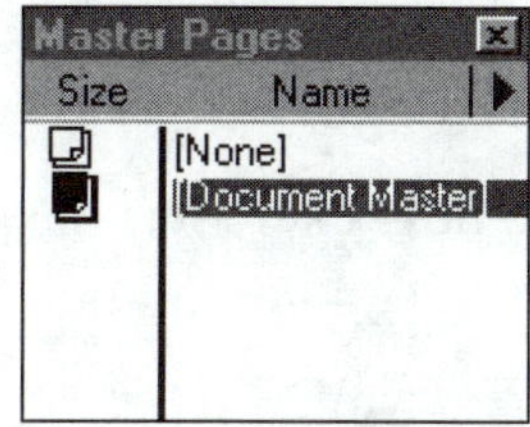

Figure 11–2 Creating specialized master pages allows you to customize pages.

- Click the arrow on the right side of the window as shown in Figure 11–2 to display commands for creating, deleting, and applying masters to specified pages.
- Click **New Master**. A Create New Master Page dialog box appears, as shown in Figure 11–3.
- Key a name for the new master page. Naming a master page, such as "Title" for a title page, helps you identify it easily. Click on the one- or two-page option. Set the margins and column guides.
- Click **OK**. Your new master page appears on the list of master pages on the Master Pages palette.

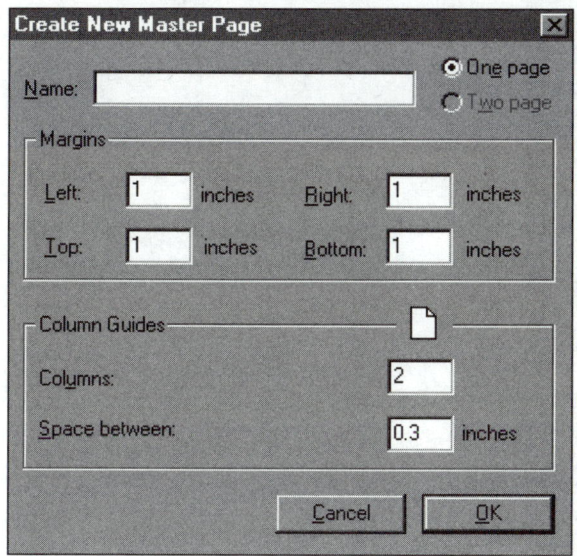

Figure 11–3 The Create New Master Page dialog box lets you customize margins and columns for the new master page.

Exercise 11–2

Create new master pages.

1. Click **Master Pages** on the Window menu.
2. Click on the menu arrow and choose **New Master**.

3. Name the new master **Cover Page**.
4. Change the number of columns to **1**. Click **OK** or **Create**.
5. Move the *Important Information* text block to the the center of the page. Enlarge the text block so it is the width of the column.
6. Click on **page 1**. In the Master Pages palette, click **Cover Page**.
7. Save the publication as **Ex11-2** and leave it open for the next exercise.

❖ DEFINING AND APPLYING STYLES

Defining and then applying styles to text gives your publication a consistent look and can save you lots of time formatting text. Any type or paragraph attributes you apply to an individual paragraph, such as typeface, size, style, alignment, indents/tabs, and hyphenation, can be applied to other paragraphs using styles. You can define new styles or modify existing ones.

To define a new style:

- Choose **Define Styles** on the Type menu. The Define Styles dialog box appears, as shown in Figure 11–4.
- Click **New**. The Edit Style dialog box appears, as shown in Figure 11–5.

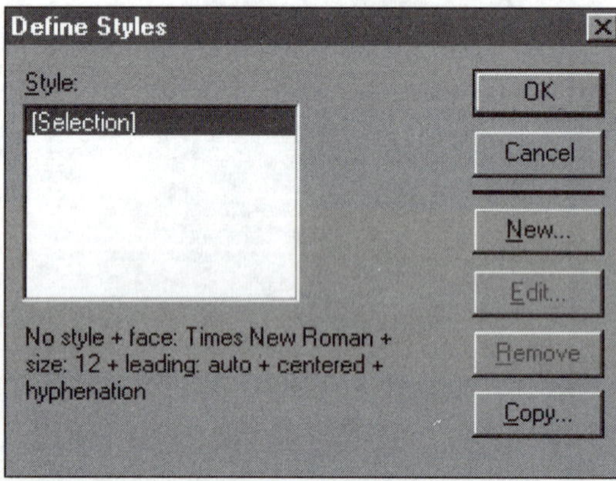

Figure 11–4 The Define Styles dialog box lists all available styles and a description of each.

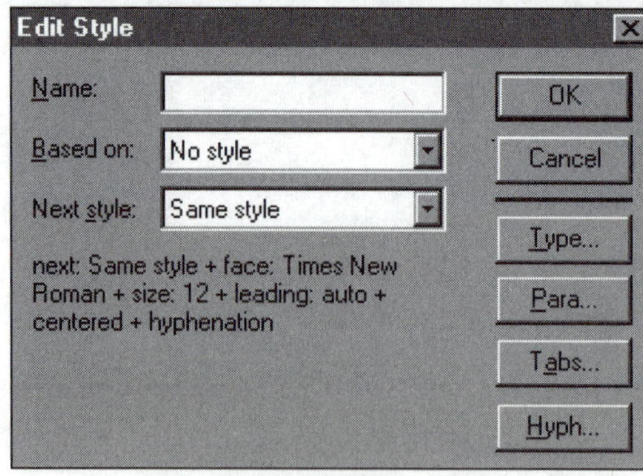

Figure 11–5 Using styles can improve the look of your publication by making it more consistent.

- Assign a name to the style. It should be a name that is descriptive of the style.
- If you want to base the new style on an existing one, click the **Based on** arrow to display a list of existing styles. Choose the style.

- Choose **Type**. A Type Specifications dialog box appears. Select the specifications. Click **OK** to return to the Edit Style dialog box.
- Choose **Para**. A Paragraph Specifications dialog box appears. Select the specifications. Click **OK** to return to the Edit Style dialog box.
- Choose **Tabs**. The Indents/Tabs dialog box appears. Select the tabs and indents. Click **OK** to return to the Edit Style dialog box.
- Choose **Hyph**. The Hyphenation dialog box appears. Select the hyphenation option. Click **OK** to return to the Edit Style dialog box.
- Click **OK** to return to the publication screen.
- To apply a style, click the Text tool anywhere in the paragraph to which you want to apply the style.
- Choose **Style** on the Type menu.
- Choose the style you want to apply to that paragraph.

To modify an existing style:

- Choose **Define Styles** on the Type menu.
- In the Define Styles dialog box, select the style you want to modify and click **Edit**. The Edit Style dialog box appears.
- Select the attributes you want to change and then click **OK** to return to the publication screen.

note

You can apply styles three ways: from the Type menu, from the Control Palette, and from the Styles Palette on the Window menu. If you use the Control Palette, the paragraph icon must be selected.

Exercise 11-3

Define styles.

1. Click the **R** master page icon. Click Document Master in the Master Pages palette.
2. Change the view to **Actual Size**. Move the text block on the pasteboard that begins with the word *Date:* so it is flush left at the top of the right column. Resize the text block so it is the width of the column.
3. Drag the text block on the pasteboard that begins with the word *To:* to the left column below the horizontal ruler guide. Resize the text block so it is the width of the column. Leave the blank lines at the top of the text block.
4. Choose **Define Styles** on the Type menu and click **New**.
5. Name the new style **Memo Form**.
6. Click **Type** and set the size to **24** point. Click the **Bold** Type style. Click **OK**.
7. Click **Para** and set the alignment to **Left**. Click **OK** to return to the Edit Style dialog box and **OK** to return to the Define Styles dialog box.
8. Create another new style named **Memo Text**. If necessary, select **Memo Form** in the Based on box.
9. Click **Type** and change the Type style to **Normal**. Click **OK**.

10. Click **Para** and change the alignment to **Right**. Click **OK** three times to return to the page.
11. Highlight the *Date* text block with the Text tool. Choose **Style** on the Type menu and apply the **Memo Form** style.
12. Highlight the lower text block.
13. Select **Style** on the Window menu to open the **Styles** palette. Apply the **Memo Form** style to the lower text block.
14. Save the publication as **Ex11-3** and leave it open for the next exercise.

❖ SETTING UP A LIBRARY PALETTE

A Library Palette is another PageMaker shortcut that lets you store graphics and text that you can quickly and easily retrieve later. You can create a Library Palette for use with a single publication or one that can be used in all your publications.

To create a new Library Palette:

- Choose **Library** on the Window menu.
- The Open Library dialog box appears. Key a name for the library in the File name text box. Because you might have several different libraries, choose a name descriptive of the contents.
- Select a file in which to save the library. Click **Open**. In Windows, a dialog box appears asking if you wish to create this file. Click **Yes**. A Library Palette appears.

To open an existing Library Palette:

- Choose **Library** on the Window menu.
- The Open Library dialog box appears.
- Locate the name of the Library Palette and click **Open**.

To open a Library from the Library Palette:

- Click the arrow in the Library Palette window. A menu appears, like that shown in Figure 11–6.
- Select **Open Library**. The Open Library dialog box appears.
- Locate the name of the Library Palette and click **Open**.

To copy a graphic or text block *to* a Library Palette:

- Choose **Library** on the Window menu and select the Library Palette to which you want to copy the object.
- Select the graphic or text block to place in the palette.

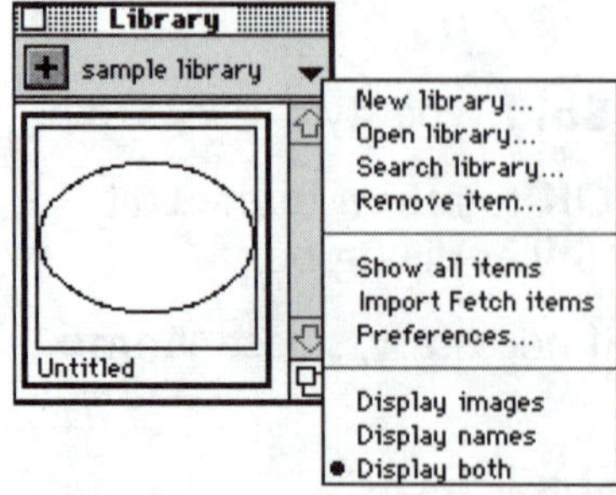

Figure 11–6 The Library Palette is an easy way to save frequently used graphics or text.

- Click the + on the Library Palette. The object appears in the palette as the last one on the list.
- Double click the object in the palette window. An Item information box appears, as shown in Figure 11–7. You may give the item a title or name, an author, a date, keywords to identify it, and a description. Click **OK**.

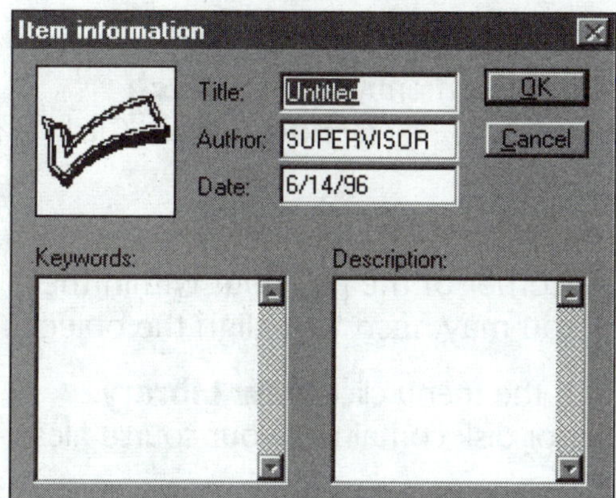

Figure 11–7 The Item information box lets you identify an object in several ways.

To copy a graphic or text block *from* a Library Palette:

- Choose **Library** on the Window menu and open the Library Palette containing the object you want to copy.
- Locate the object and drag it from the palette window to the publication. A Library graphic icon appears. When you release the mouse button, the object appears on the screen.

To search a Library Palette for a particular object:

- Click the arrow in the palette and choose **Search Library** from the menu. A search dialog box appears, like that shown in Figure 11–8.
- Search by keyword, author, or name (Macintosh) or title (Windows). You may search combining two keywords using *and*, *or*, and *but not* by clicking on the One keyword only arrow.

note

You can resize a palette by dragging the side or bottom margins (Windows) or by using the resizing box (Macintosh).

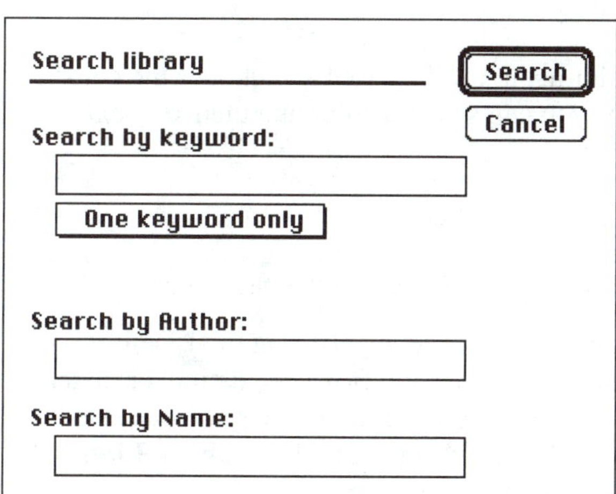

Figure 11-8 Search Library dialog box

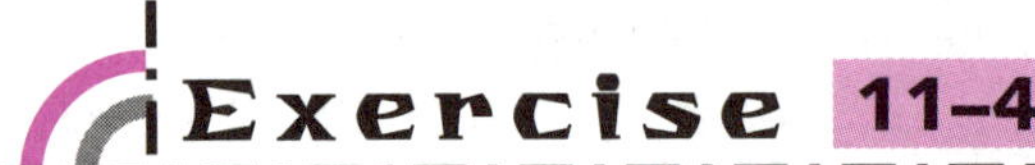

Exercise 11-4

Use the Library Palette.

1. Choose **Library** on the Window menu. Select the folder or disk containing the template files and choose the file named **Graphics**. Click **Open**.
2. Click the arrow on the Library Palette. From the menu, select **Search Library**. In the Search by title or name text box, key **School Logo**. Click **Search**.
3. The graphic appears in the Library Palette. Drag the *School Logo* object from the Library Palette to the upper left corner of the page but within the margins. **Click** on the publication page. You may need to realign the object.
4. Click the arrow on the Library Palette. From the menu click **New Library**. Save the library as **Lesson11** to the folder or disk containing your course files.
5. Use the Pointer tool to select the check mark located on the pasteboard. Click the **+** on the Library palette to add the object to the Library. When the check mark appears in the palette, double click on it to open the Item information dialog box. Name the object **Checkmark**. Click **OK**.
6. Click the **Close** box on the Library Palette.
7. Save the publication as **Ex11-4** and leave it open for the next exercise.

❖ USING THE COLORS PALETTE

Using color is a quick way to add interest to any publication. Color can be assigned easily to text or to graphics created in PageMaker using the Colors palette opened from the Window menu. If you are using a monochrome monitor, you will see shades of gray.

note

If you assign color to graphics that you import into a publication, you will be able to use only a single color for any printed area.

To use the Colors palette with text:

- Choose **Colors** on the Window menu. The Colors Palette opens, as shown in Figure 11–9.
- Highlight the text to be assigned color using the Text tool and choose the color you want from the Colors palette, or you can select a color and then key text.

To use the Colors Palette with a graphic:

- Choose **Colors** on the Window menu.
- Select the graphic with the Pointer tool and then click on the new color.
- You can change the color of the border of a graphic by clicking the Line box (see Figure 11–9). Change the interior color using the Box designation, or match both the line and the interior color by selecting the Both box. Or you can select a color for the line, the box, or both and then draw the graphic with the **Line**, **Constrained Line**, **Rectangle, Polygon**, or **Ellipse tool**.

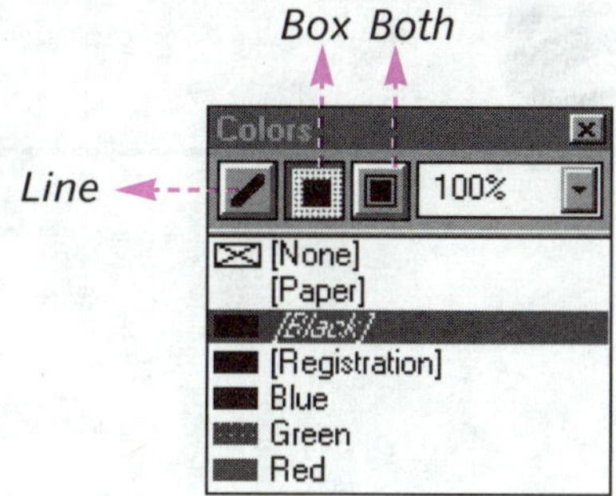

Figure 11–9 PageMaker lets you change the colors of figures created with the drawing tools.

Exercise 11–5

Use the Colors Palette.

1. Choose **Colors** on the Window menu.
2. Highlight *Copper High School* in the logo.
3. Assign it the color blue (or a shade of gray).
4. Select the top line of the crossroads in the school logo. Color it red (or another shade of gray).
5. Select the left vertical line. Color it blue (or another shade of gray).
6. Change the color of the text "*Where All Worlds Meet.*" to red (or a shade of gray).
7. Draw a green (or another shade of gray) line below the motto that cuts through the two vertical lines.
8. Save the publication as **Ex11-5**.
9. Print all the pages in the publication and then close it.

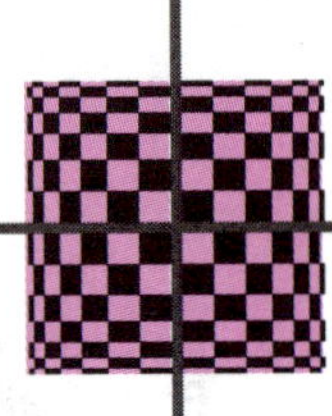

activities

❖ TRUE/FALSE

On the blank line before each sentence, place a **T** *if the statement is true and an* **F** *if it is false.*

____ 1. When you want an object to appear on every page of your publication, you have to add it only once to the master pages.

____ 2. The only rulers and guides you can use on a master page are column guides.

____ 3. The Master Pages Palette is used to create different master pages within the same publication.

____ 4. Defining a style applies text and paragraph attributes to individual words.

____ 5. A Library Palette stores frequently used graphics and text.

❖ COMPLETION

Answer the questions below in the space provided.

6. How can pages be numbered automatically?

____

____

7. What are at least three attributes you can assign when defining styles?

____

____

8. What is the process for creating a new master page?

____

____

9. What options do you have when searching the Library Palette?

____

____

10. What limitations do you have when applying color to an imported graphic?

____

____

Review Exercise 11-1

Use PageMaker shortcuts.

1. Open **Memoform** from the template files.
2. In Document Setup, change the number of pages to **2 double-sided** but not facing pages. Click **OK**.
3. Select the **right** Master Page icon and copy the footer.
4. Select the **left** Master Page icon and paste the footer below the bottom margin. Create **3** columns on this page with **.5** inches between them. (*Hint*: Use **Column Guides** on the Layout menu.)
5. Place horizontal ruler guides at the **2**-, **3**-, **4**-, **5**-, **6**-, **7**-, and **8**-inch marks. **Lock** guides. (*Hint:* Use **Lock Guides** on the **Guides and Rulers** submenu on the Layout menu.)
6. Return to **page 1**. Start a new text block on the pasteboard and enter **September 14**. Press **Enter** or **Return** three times. Key **Immediately**. Assign the style **Memo Text** to *September 14* and *Immediately.* Move the text block so that the text is aligned across from *Date*: and *Action Date:*.
7. Key **Faculty and Staff** in a new text block. Press **Enter** or **Return** three times. Key **J. S. Potts**. Press **Enter** or **Return** three times. Key **School Closings**. Assign the style **Memo Text** to this text. Change the size of the text to **18 point**. Align the text block so that *Faculty and Staff*, *J. S. Potts*, and *School Closings* appears below the titles *To:*, *From:*, and *Re:*.
8. Define a new style. Name it **Memo Copy**. It should be based on **No style**. The style should be **10-point Times** or **Times New Roman, normal** style, and **left alignment**. Return to your page.
9. Drag the text on the pasteboard into the right column below the ruler guide. Make sure to display all text and adjust the width of the text block to fit the column. Assign the style **Memo Copy** to all the paragraphs of text.
10. Edit the style Memo Copy. Change it to **14 point** with **hyphenation off**. Assign a Paragraph space of **.2 inches After**.
11. Assign the color **red** (or a shade of gray) to the second paragraph of the text block. It begins with *It is important . . . .*
12. Go to page **2**.

13. Open the **Library** Palette named *Graphics.* Search for the graphic named **box** and drag it from the Library Palette to the page so that the top of the box is on the 2-inch ruler guide and its left side is on the left margin.

14. Copy the box. Paste it five times so the boxes are in a vertical line and within the borders established by the guides, as shown in Figure 11–10. (*Hint*: You can use **Multiple Paste** on the Edit menu. Set the horizontal offset at **0** and the vertical at **1** inch.)

15. Select the column of boxes. (Hold down the **Shift** key and click on each box.) Copy them and paste them in the second and third columns so the top side of each column is on the 2-inch ruler guide.

16. Draw a blue (or another shade of gray) **2pt** line down the first column, as shown in Figure 11–10. Send it to the back. Do the same in columns 2 and 3.

17. Draw a red (or another shade of gray) **4pt** line across the top boxes, as shown in Figure 11–10. Send it to the back.

18. Drag the text block titled *column 1* from the Library Palette to the first column. Center the text within the boxes. Do the same for columns 2 and 3 using the text blocks titled *column 2* and *column 3* from the Library Palette.

19. Save the publication as **Re11-1**.

20. Print all the pages in the publication, close it, and end your PageMaker session.

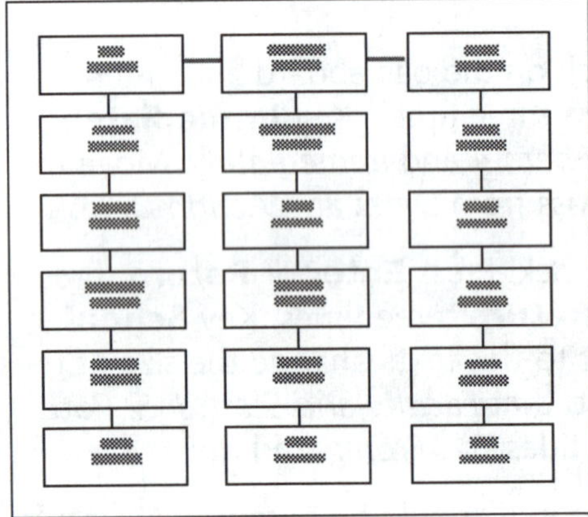

Figure 11–10

Applying Desktop Publishing Skills

❖ OBJECTIVES

Upon completion of this lesson, you will be able to:

1. Create a logo.
2. Design a letterhead.
3. Plan a poster.
4. Set up a business card.
5. Design a certificate.
6. Plan an invitation.
7. Create a program.

Estimated Time: 1 hour

❖ INTRODUCTION

By working through the previous lessons of this book, you have developed PageMaker skills. In this lesson, you will apply what you have learned by completing a desktop publishing center simulation.

❖ CREATING A LOGO

We see logos everyday—on TV, on the clothes we wear, on the food we buy. Logos are a symbol, icon, or image that quickly identifies an organization. You can combine text and graphics to create a logo. A sample logo is shown in Figure 12–1.

Exercise 12–1

Let's assume that you are operating a desktop publishing center. Create an original logo for the DTP Center. Include your name as part of the logo.

1. Create a logo using the drawing and text tools.
2. Copy the logo to the Logos Library Palette. You might want to group the various elements of your logo. Use your name to identify the logo in the palette.

Figure 12–1
A logo can be an important way to identify an organization.

3. Save the file as **Logo** to the folder or disk containing your course files.
4. Print the logo and close the publication.

❖ DESIGNING A LETTERHEAD

A letterhead usually consists of an organization's logo, name, address, telephone number, fax number, and Internet address and is used on company stationery. A sample letterhead is shown in Figure 12–2.

Figure 12–2
A letterhead can be designed in a variety of ways as long as the essential information is included.

Exercise 12–2

Create an original letterhead for the DTP Center.

1. Start a new publication. Use the logo you created in the last exercise as part of your letterhead.
2. Save the file as **Letter**.
3. Print the letterhead and close the publication.

❖ PLANNING A POSTER

Posters can be any size or shape, although it should be possible to read posters at a minimum distance of 10 feet. When designing a poster, you need to include all the information necessary to convey your message. A sample poster is shown in Figure 12–3.

SENIOR HIGH BANQUET

March 19 6:30 p.m.

Elegant Steakhouse
9701 Ave. G

Ticket Price: $9 Tickets go on sale January 10.

Figure 12–3
Big type and graphics can make posters more appealing to the reader.

Exercise 12–3

Create a poster.

1. Start a new publication and create a poster using the following information:

```
Senior High Banquet
March 19 6:30 p.m.
Elegant Steakhouse
9701 Ave G.
$9 a ticket
Tickets go on sale January 10
```

2. Save the file as **Poster**.
3. Print the poster and close the publication.

❖ SETTING UP A BUSINESS CARD

Business cards are used to promote a business and the people who work in it. A standard business card is 3½ inches wide by 2 inches tall. An example of a business card is shown in Figure 12–4. A business card usually includes a logo, business name, name and job title of the employee, address of the business, phone number, fax number, and E-mail address.

Desktop
Publishing
Center

Ashley Barfield

Lincoln High Room 215
(515) 555-4567 FAX (515) 555-7654
ashbar@lhs.edu

Figure 12–4
Many desktop publishing businesses produce business cards.

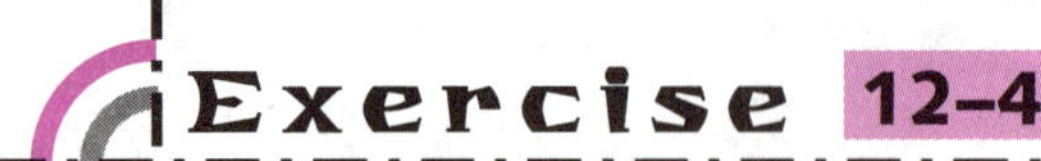

Exercise 12-4

Design a business card for the DTP Center.

1. Start a new publication and use ruler guides to set off a space that's 3½ inches wide by 2 inches tall.
2. Use your logo and add any other graphics and text to the business card.
3. Save the file as **Buscard**.
4. Print the business card and close the publication.

❖ DESIGNING A CERTIFICATE

Certificates usually include ornate borders and might look something like Figure 12–5.

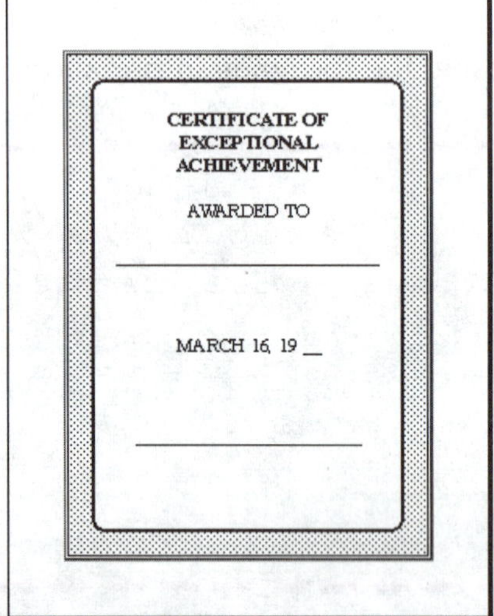

Figure 12–5
Design a certificate using different types of borders.

Exercise 12-5

Design a certificate.

1. Start a new publication and design a certificate for Exceptional Achievement. Refer to Figure 12-5 for other information to include on the certificate. Include an interesting border.
2. Save the file as **Certif**.
3. Print the certificate and close the publication.

❖ PLANNING AN INVITATION

To create an invitation like the one shown in Figure 12–6, fold a piece of paper first and identify where you want elements of the invitation to appear. When you print it out, all you'll have to do is fold it. You'll find that PageMaker's rotation feature comes in handy when designing invitations.

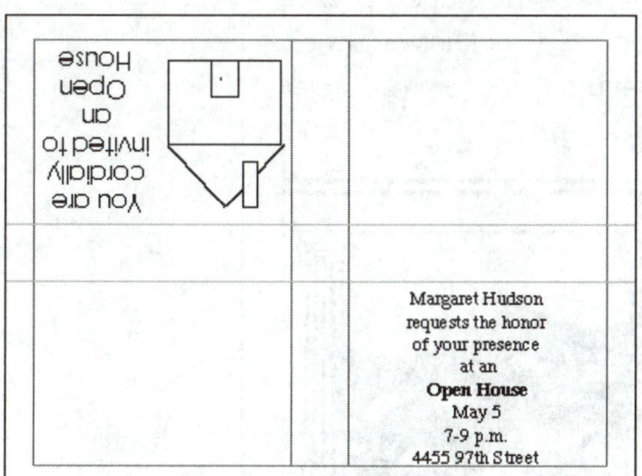

Figure 12–6
Plan your invitation first using a piece of paper.

Exercise 12–6

Design an invitation.

1. Start a new publication and change the orientation to wide. Use the drawing tools to create a graphic for your invitation. Then include the following information:

```
Margaret Hudson

Open House

4455 97th Street

May 5

7 - 9 p.m.

no RSVP is needed
```

2. Save the file as **Openinv**.
3. Print the invitation and close the publication.

❖ CREATING A PROGRAM

A program for a special event can follow a variety of formats, but one that's commonly used is illustrated in Figure 12–7. This example was created as a two-page document using wide (or landscape) orientation. Each page has two columns that represent a full page of the program when it's printed and folded. Again, it is helpful to use paper to determine what elements are to appear on each side and portion of the sheet before you start a PageMaker publication.

Cast	Director .... Billy Tolman
Leigh Welch	Stage Crew .... Roy Drexer
Bruce Gott	Props .... Missy Harmon
Chris Sivo	Makeup .... Tommy Eppler
Kristen Lynam	
Tracy Phipps	

Program Designed
by Students
in the
PageMaker
Desktop Publishing Class
Room 218
(515) 555-4567

Mark White's

The Harmonious Jangle
of Sound

Presented by
the Choir
and
Drama Students
of Lincoln High School

Friday, October 26, 19 __
Saturday, October 27, 19 __
8:15 p.m.

Figure 12–7
Change orientation to print out programs of varying sizes.

Exercise 12–7

Design a program.

1. Start a new publication and create a program. Change the orientation to wide. Each page should have two columns with 1.5 inches of space between them.
2. Place the following information in the program:

Front cover:

Mark White's The Harmonious Jangle of Sound

Presented by the Choir and Drama Students of Lincoln High School

Friday, October 26, 19 __

Saturday, October 27, 19 __

8:15 p.m.

Inside front cover:

Cast - Leigh Welch, Bruce Gott, Chris Sivo, Kristen Lynam, and Tracy Phipps

Inside back cover:

Director - Billy Tolman

Stage Crew - Roy Drexer

Props - Missy Harmon

Makeup - Tommy Eppler

Back cover:

Program Designed by the PageMaker Desktop Publishing Class

Room 218

(515) 555-4567

3. Save the file as **Program**.
4. Print the program and close the publication.

❖ DESKTOP PUBLISHING IN YOUR FUTURE

You are now an experienced desktop publisher. You can design documents such as newsletters, brochures, programs, handbooks, business forms, and flyers to communicate messages effectively. These new skills increase your ability to find jobs in the future. Organizations that use desktop publishing are diverse. They include government agencies, churches, newspapers, advertising agencies, colleges, volunteer services, publishing companies, and hospitals. Both small and large businesses use desktop publishing.

Regardless of where you work, your desktop publishing skills will be an asset. Good luck!

Advanced PageMaker Features

This appendix summarizes some of PageMaker 6.0's advanced desktop publishing capabilities.

❖ SETTING UP A TABLE OF CONTENTS

If you create a long publication such as a pamphlet or even a book, your reader will find a table of contents helpful. With PageMaker you can create a table of contents with surprising ease and professionalism using the Create TOC command on the Utilities menu.

To set up a table of contents:

- Select **Define Styles** on the Type menu. Select the style that represents the heading level you want to use for the table of contents. Usually, it includes those that represent the headings. Click **Edit**. Click **Para**. Click **include in table of contents** under the Options. Return to the Define Styles dialog box.
- If you wish to include more than one style, select the next style and follow the same procedure. When you have identified all the styles to include in the table of contents, click **OK** to return to the screen.
- If necessary, insert a new page at the beginning of your publication for your table of contents.
- Select **Create TOC** on the Utilities menu.
- A Create Table of Contents dialog box appears, as shown in Figure AP–1. Key the title. Click **OK**. A text icon appears. Click on the page created for your table of contents.
- Once the table of contents is in place, a TOC style is listed in your Style menu. You can edit the type attributes of these styles just as you do other styles.

Figure AP–1
The Create Table of Contents dialog box lets you determine the name given to your table of contents.

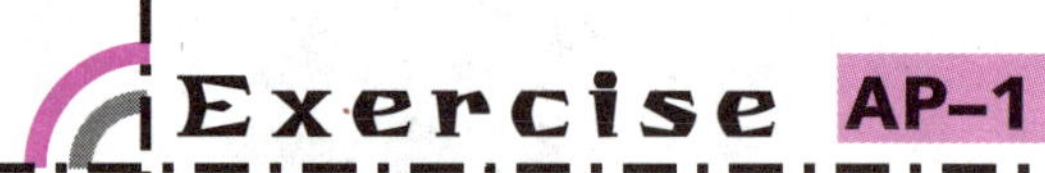

Create a table of contents.

1. Open **Doc** from the template files. If necessary, click page **2** and change the view so you can read the headings.
2. Select **Define Styles** on the Type menu. Select the style **Subhead1**, which has been applied to the two main subheads in the text. Click **Edit**. Click **Para**. Click **Include in table of contents** under the Options. Click **OK** three times to return to the screen.
3. Move to **page 1**.
4. Select **Create TOC** on the Utilities menu. Key the title **Table of Contents**. Click **OK**. Click the text icon at the top of page 1.
5. Select **Define Styles** on the Type menu and then select **TOC Subhead1**. Click **Edit** and change the type to **14** point **Normal** style. Click **OK**. The two main subheads and the page numbers that they appear on should be displayed on the table of contents page.
6. Save the publication as **Exap-1** to the folder or disk containing your course files and then leave it open for the next exercise.

❖ ESTABLISHING AN INDEX

Just as a table of contents is useful in referencing topics in a publication, so is an index. You can create an index for a book using the Create Index command on the Utilities menu.

To establish an index:

- Highlight a word that you wish to include in the index. Select **Index Entry** on the Utilities menu. An Add Index Entry dialog box appears as shown in Figure AP–2. Click **OK**.

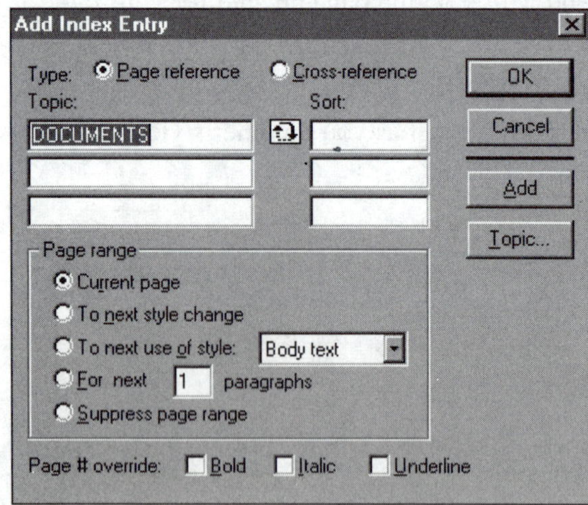

Figure AP–2 The Add Index Entry dialog box lets you add words to an index.

- If necessary, insert a new page at the end of your publication for your index.
- Select **Create Index** on the Utilities menu.
- A Create Index dialog box appears, as shown in Figure AP–3. Key the title. Click **OK**. A text icon appears. Click the icon at the top of the page created for your index. Once the index is in place, you can change any of its type attributes.

Figure AP–3
The Create Index dialog box lets you name an index.

Exercise AP–2

Create an index.

1. On page **2**, highlight the boldface words **Saddle stitching**. Select **Index Entry** on the Utilities menu. In the Add Index Entry dialog box, capitalize the word *stitching* in the Topic box. Click **OK**.
2. Highlight the other boldface words: *Mechanical Binding*, *single-sided*, and *double-sided*. Capitalize the first letter of each word added to the Index.
3. Move to page **4**.
4. Select **Create Index** on the Utilities menu. When the Create Index dialog box appears, click **OK**. Click the text icon at the top of page 4.
5. Save the publication as **Exap-2**, print it, and then leave it open for the next exercise.

CREATING AN ADOBE PDF FILE

In today's world, the publication process is no longer limited to print. Electronic media are becoming important means of publishing. With PageMaker, you can publish electronically using Adobe PDF (Portable Document Format), which allows those without PageMaker to read and use your publications.

Creating PDF files requires that Adobe Acrobat and Adobe Distiller be installed on your system. Distiller is opened when you select Create Adobe PDF on the File menu. It "distills" the essence of your PageMaker publication, changing it to a PDF file. Adobe Acrobat is used to read PDF files that you have distilled. Acrobat and Distiller come on the PageMaker 6.0 CD-ROM.

To create a PDF file:

- Select **Create Adobe PDF** on the File menu. You must have Adobe Distiller installed from the PageMaker 6.0 CD-ROM. A Create Adobe PDF dialog box appears, as shown in Figure AP–4.
- Click **Create**.

- A Save As dialog box appears. The file name under which you have saved the original file is given as the default. You can change the name if you want. Click **Save**. PageMaker launches Distiller to create the PDF file.
- Open **Adobe Acrobat** to read the PDF file. In Windows, click the Start button on the taskbar and then open the Programs folder. Acrobat should be in the Adobe folder. Macintosh users open the Adobe folder in the Applications folder on the desktop.

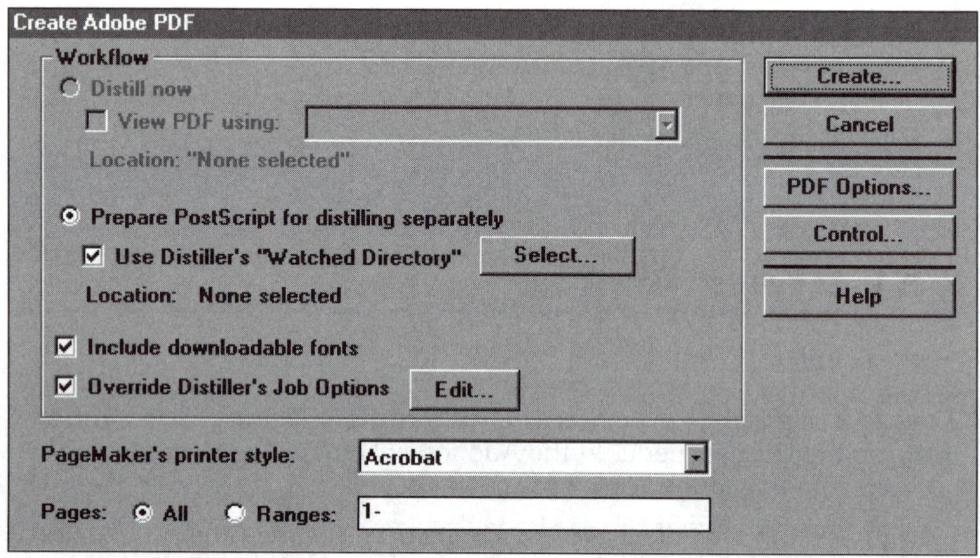

Figure AP–4
The Create Adobe PDF dialog box is the first step in creating a file that can be read by others without PageMaker.

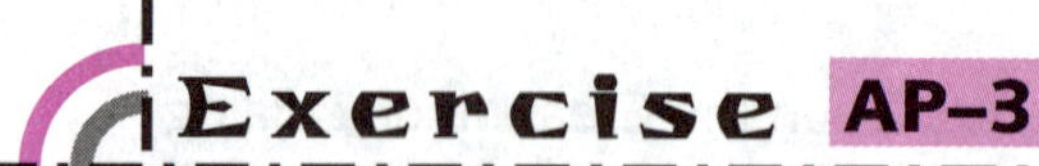

Create a PDF file.

1. Select **Create Adobe PDF** on the File menu. A message box might appear asking if you want to save this document. Click **No**.
2. When the Create Adobe PDF dialog box appears, make sure that the **Distill now** option is selected. Click **Create**.
3. When the Save As dialog box appears, change the file name to **Exap-3** and save it to the folder or disk containing your course files. Click **Save**. The Distiller screen appears. When you return to the PageMaker screen, close PageMaker without saving any changes. Close Distiller.
4. From the **Programs** folder (Windows) or the **Applications** folder (Macintosh), open **Acrobat Reader.**
5. From the Open dialog box, select the Acrobat file **Exap-3** from your course files. Click **OK** or **Open** to read the file.
6. Select **Exit** or **Quit** on the File menu to end your Acrobat session.

❖ CREATING HTML PAGES

You can convert PageMaker publications to Hypertext Markup Language (HTML) documents that can be published on the Internet, the worldwide "network of networks." You can navigate the Internet through the World-Wide Web—a graphical system of links and pointers that connects Web sites (individual network or user locations) and documents that are on the Internet. When you access a Web site, you can view its Web pages, which are single screens of data compiled by individual Internet users.

Reading HTML documents requires the use of a web browser—a program that lets you read Web pages. If you have Windows 95, you can use the Internet Explorer, which comes with your operating system. If you are using Macintosh, you will have to use a browser such as Netscape.

You can convert PageMaker stories, pages, or an entire publication to HTML documents that can be published on the World-Wide Web by using the HTML Author plug-in.

To create an HTML document:

- Choose the **Utilities** menu, then **PageMaker Plug-ins**, and then **HTML Author**.
- In the HTML Author dialog box, click **Contents**, and then click **New**. The New HTML Document dialog box appears, as shown in Figure AP–5.
- Choose **PageMaker Pages** to define a page or range of pages to be exported as HTML, or **Stories** to define a story or set of stories. Enter a document title and then click **Next**.
- In the Assign dialog box, choose which pages or stories should be exported into the HTML document and then click **Next**. The order in which you add pages or stories is the order in which they will be exported.
- In the Location dialog box, select the location to which you want the HTML document to be created and give it a filename. Click **OK**. You are returned to the HTML Author Contents dialog box.
- Click **Export HTML** to create the HTML document. Click **OK** to return to the PageMaker screen.

Figure AP–5 Define the pages or stories to be added to the HTML document in the New HTML Document dialog box.

UNDERSTANDING LINKS AND ANCHORS

If you've ever "surfed the net," you've probably used links to jump to another part of the Web page you're reading, to move to another page completely, or to retrieve information from another computer. You can create such links in your HTML documents using the hypertext link feature. You use the HTML Author plug-in to create up to 50 links in a publication. When you create a link, the HTML Author stores the linked information inside the PageMaker publication.

The destination of the link is called the *anchor.* You can have up to 50 anchors in a PageMaker publication.

To create an anchor:

- Select the text you want to define as an anchor.
- On the Utilities menu, select **PageMaker Plug-ins** and then **HTML Author**.
- Click the **Create Links** tab (see Figure AP–6), choose **Anchor** from the Create menu, enter a label for the anchor, and then click **Create**.
- Click **OK** to close the dialog box.

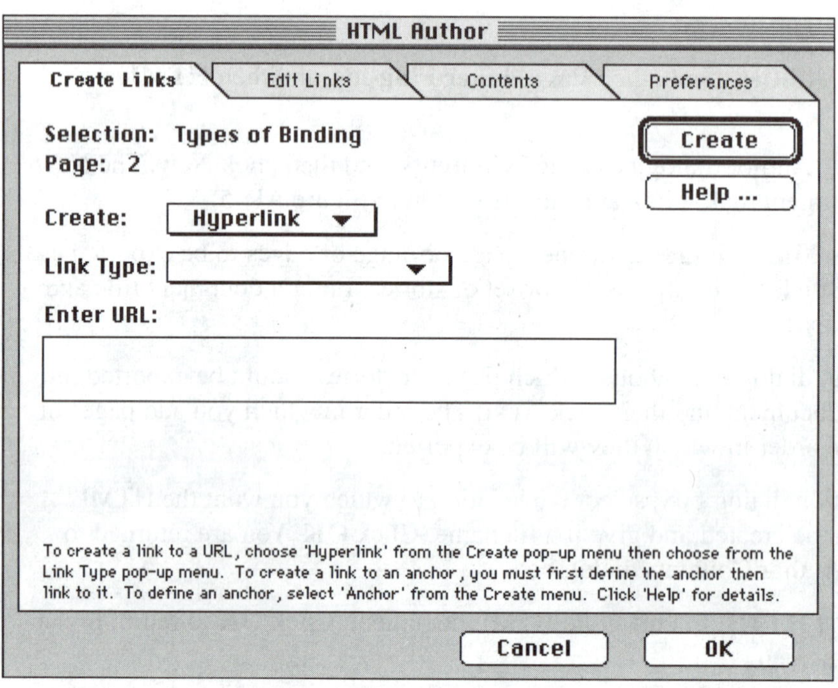

Figure AP–6
Establish links and anchors in the Create Links tab in the HTML Author dialog box.

To create a link to an anchor:

- Select the text or graphic to which you want to attach a link.
- On the Utilities menu, select **PageMaker Plug-ins** and then **HTML Author**.
- Select the **Create Links** tab. Make sure that **Hyperlink** is selected in the Create submenu, and then choose **Link to Anchor** from the Link Type menu.
- Select an anchor from the list and then click **Create**.
- Click **OK** to close the HTML Author dialog box.

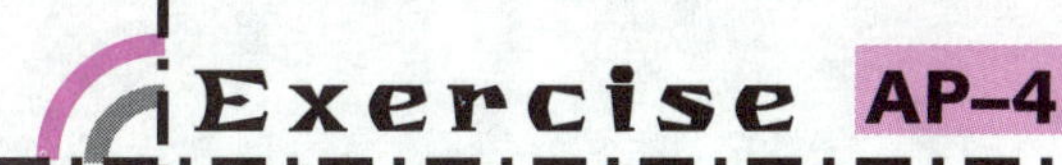

Exercise AP-4

Create an HTML document.

1. Open **Exap-2** from the folder or disk containing your course files.
2. Highlight the words **Types of Binding** on page 2 of the document. You'll define this as an anchor.
3. Select **PageMaker Plug-ins** on the Utilities menu. Choose **HTML Author** on the submenu. In the Create Links tab of the HTML Author dialog box, select **Anchor** from the Create box. Key **Binding** as a label for the anchor. Click **Create**. Click **OK**.
4. Highlight **Planning the Margins** on page 3. Create an HTML anchor named **Margins** for it.
5. In the Table of Contents on page 1, highlight the words **Types of Binding**.
6. Select **PageMaker Plug-ins** on the Utilities menu. Choose **HTML Author** on the submenu. In the Create box, select **Hyperlink**. Click the arrow on the Link Type box and select **Link to Anchor**. Choose **Binding** as the anchor. Click **Create**. Click **OK**.
7. Highlight **Planning the Margins** in the Table of Contents. Create a link to **Margins** for it. Deselect **Planning the Margins**.
8. Select **PageMaker Plug-ins** on the Utilities menu. Choose **HTML Author** on the submenu. Click the **Contents** tab. Click **New**. Choose the **Stories** option and name the document **Exap-4**. Click **Next**.
9. Click **MULTIPAGE DOCUMENTS** in the Unassigned list and then click **Add**. Click **Table of Contents** and then click **Add**. Click **Index** and click **Add**. Click **Next**. Save the file as **Exap-4** to the folder or disk containing your course files. Click **OK**.
10. Click **Export HTML**. Click **OK**. When you return to the PageMaker screen, save the document as **Exap-4a**. Close the publication.
11. Use a web browser to read your file.

review

Review Exercise AP-1

Use PageMaker's table of contents and indexing features.

1. Open **Booklet** from the template files.
2. From **Define Styles** on the Type menu, select the style **Headline**. Edit the paragraph specifications to include the style in the table of contents. Return to the Define Styles dialog box.
3. Select the style Subhead. Follow the procedures above and include Subhead in your table of contents. Return to the publication.
4. Create a table of contents and place it on page 2.
5. Edit the **TOC Headline** to **12** point **Normal** style. Edit the **TOC Subhead** to **12** point **Normal** style indented .5 inches.
6. Beginning on page 3, add all bold and underlined text (except for subheadings) to the index. Change the first letter of any entries that are lower case to upper case.
7. Create two columns on the last page. (*Hint:* Select **Column Guides** on the Layout menu. Set both sides separately.)
8. Create an index and place it on the last page. Flow the text so the title is centered on the page and the index entries are in two columns.
9. Save the publication as **Reap-1**.
10. Print the publication and leave it open for the next exercise.

Review Exercise AP-2

Create a PDF file.

1. Select **Create Adobe PDF** on the File menu. Click **Create**.
2. When the Save As dialog box appears, change the file name to **Reap-2**. Click **Save**.
3. When you return to the PageMaker screen, save your publication as **Reap-2a** and close it.
4. Open **Adobe Acrobat** to read the PDF file.

Review Exercise AP-3

Create an HTML document.

1. The gif file labeled **Logo1** must be copied to the folder or disk containing your course files. Your instructor can help you with this.
2. Open **NewBook** from the template files.
3. From the File menu, place the the graphic **Logo1.gif** in the center of page 1.
4. Highlight the word **OVERVIEW** on page 3 of the document.
5. From the **PageMaker Plug-ins** on the Utilities menu, choose **HTML Author**. Create an anchor called **Overview**. Create anchors for the words **TECHNOLOGY**, **FONTS** (page 5), **LAYOUT** (page 6), and **CONCLUSION** (page 8), using those words as the anchor labels.
6. Highlight **OVERVIEW** in the Table of Contents on page 2.
7. From the **PageMaker Plug-ins** on the Utilities menu, choose **HTML Author**. Create a link to Overview. Create links from **TECHNOLOGY** to **Technology**, from **FONTS** to **Fonts**, from **LAYOUT** to **Layout**, and from **CONCLUSION** to **Conclusion**.
8. From the **PageMaker Plug-ins** on the Utilities menu, choose **HTML Author**. From the Contents tab, click **New**. Select **PageMaker Pages** and name the document **Reap-3**. Click **Next**.
9. Click **Add All**. Click **Next**. Save the file as **Reap-3** to the folder or disk containing your course files. Click **OK**.
10. Click **Export HTML**. Click **OK**.
11. When you return to the PageMaker screen, save your publication as **Reap-3a** and end your PageMaker session. Use a web browser to read your HTML file.

index

A

B

C

D

E

index

index

index

index

notes

notes

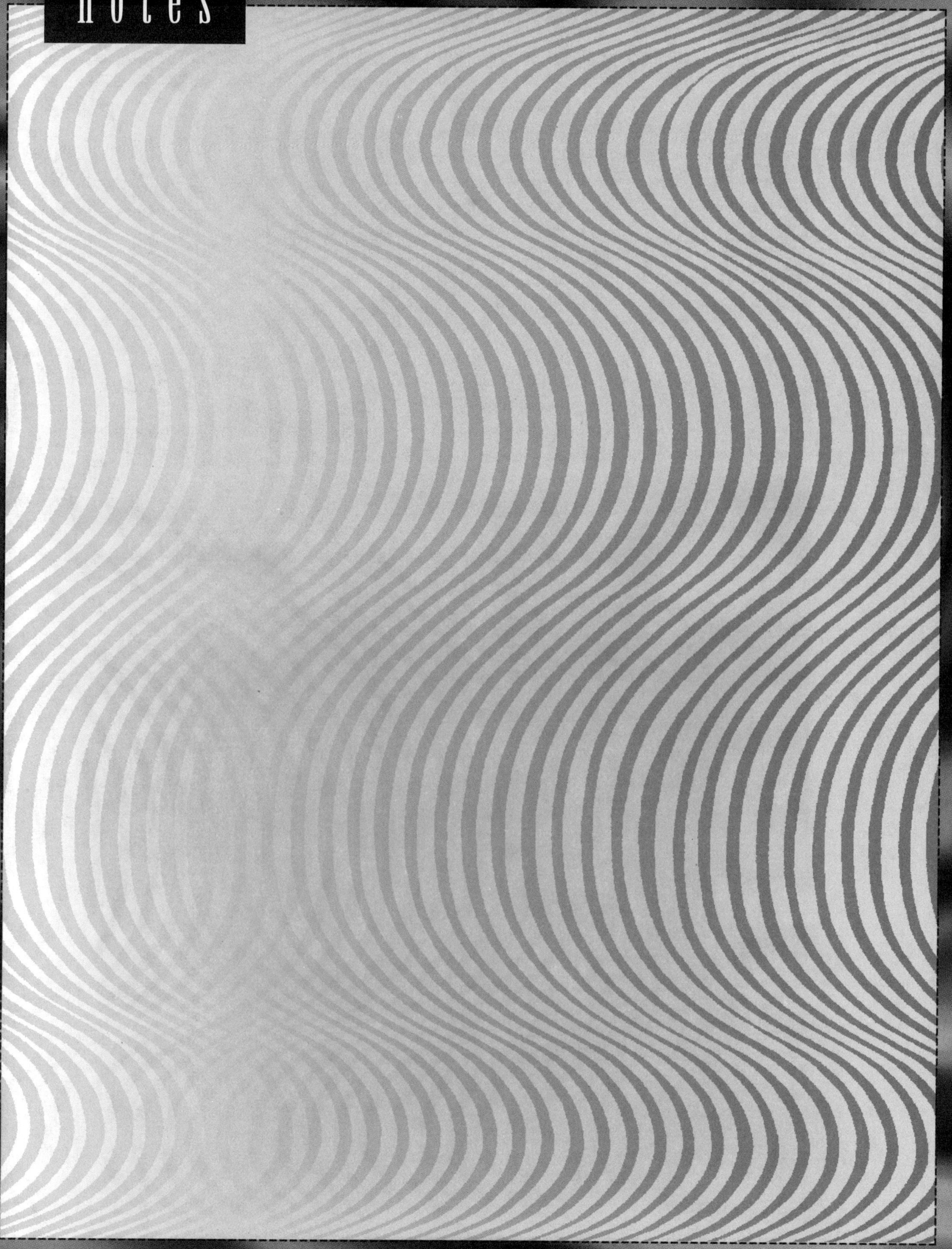

notes